CLAIMING MY PLACE

Sura Gitla Gomolinska, nicknamed Gucia, at age twenty-one in Kraków, Poland, 1937

Planaria Price
with Helen Reichmann West

CLAIMING MY PLACE

Coming of Age in the Shadow of the Holocaust

Farrar Straus Giroux
New York

Farrar Straus Giroux Books for Young Readers
An imprint of Macmillan Publishing Group, LLC
175 Fifth Avenue, New York, NY 10010

Copyright © 2018 by Planaria Price and Helen Reichmann West
Maps © 2018 by ElkingtonDesignWorks
All rights reserved
Printed in the United States of America
Designed by Roberta Pressel
First edition, 2018
1 3 5 7 9 10 8 6 4 2

fiercereads.com

Library of Congress Cataloging-in-Publication Data

Names: Price, Planaria J., author. | West, Helen Reichmann, author.
Title: Claiming my place : coming of age in the shadow of the Holocaust / Planaria Price ;
    with Helen Reichmann West.
Description: First edition. | New York, NY : Farrar Straus Giroux, 2018
Identifiers: LCCN 2017023580 | ISBN 9780374305291 (hardcover)
Subjects: LCSH: Reichmann, Barbara, 1916–2007—Juvenile literature. | Jews—Poland—Piotrków
    Trybunalski—Biography—Juvenile literature. | Holocaust, Jewish (1939–1945)—
Poland—Biography—Juvenile literature.
Classification: LCC DS134.72.R447 P75 2018 | DDC 940.53/18092 [B]—dc23
LC record available at https://lccn.loc.gov/2017023580

Our books may be purchased in bulk for promotional, educational, or business use.
Please contact your local bookseller or the Macmillan Corporate and Premium Sales Department
at (800) 221-7945, ext. 5442, or by e-mail at MacmillanSpecialMarkets@macmillan.com.

For the Six Million,
whose stories can never be shared,
and for Sabina
—P.P.

For Hendla Gomolinska and Chaya Lau,
two strong, independent women who paved the way
—H.R.W.

Now go write it down on a tablet
And inscribe it in a record,
That it may be with them for future days,
A witness forever.
—Isaiah 30:8

CONTENTS

PHOTOGRAPHS

MAPS

LIST OF CHARACTERS

Sura Gitla Gomolinska, born May 15, 1916, nicknamed **Gucia,** changed her name in 1942 to **Danuta Barbara Tanska,** nicknamed **Basia.** Barbara/Basia were the names she kept for the rest of her life.

GOMOLINSKI FAMILY

Itzak Hirsch Gomolinski (father, known to his children as **Tatte**)
Hendla Libeskind Gomolinska (mother)
Hela (**Jacob Brem,** husband; **Marek Brem,** son; **Abek Brem,** brother-in-law)
Chanusck
Sura Gitla (**Gucia,** later known as **Basia**)
Idek
Josek
Beniek
Rifka
Regina

OTHER FAMILIES FEATURED IN THE STORY

Uncle Josef Libeskind (Hendla's brother, Basia's uncle)
Aunt Sura Libeskind
Janek
Mala
Mania
Mendel
Moshe
Rozia

Uncle Mendel Libeskind (Hendla's brother, Basia's uncle)
Aunt Sprintza Libeskind
Elkanah
Hinda

Rabbi Moshe Chaim Lau (chief rabbi in Piotrków beginning in
    1934)
Rebbitzin Chaya Lau
Naphtali (Tulek)
Shmuel Yitzhak (Milek)
Yisrael (Lulek)

Baila Reichmann (Leon Reichmann's mother)
Leon Reichmann (Basia's husband)
Abraham Reichmann (Leon Reichmann's brother)
Henry Marton (Leon Reichmann's cousin)

Heniek Wajshof (Basia's high school boyfriend)
Mania and **Dora Wajshof** (Heniek Wajshof's sisters)
Srulek Wajshof (Heniek Wajshof's cousin)

OTHER MAIN CHARACTERS

Chana Chojnacka (Gomolinski family's Jewish maid)
Herr and Frau Schweibold (owners of Ulm hotel where Basia
    worked)
Itka Ber (Basia's childhood friend)
Itka Moskowitz (Basia's college roommate)
Janova (Gomolinski family's Polish maid)
Kazimierz Dobranski (Polish neighbor)
Krysia (Gomolinski family's Polish maid)
Maya (Gucia's friend and fellow worker at Ulm hotel)
Rozia Nissenson (Basia's school friend)
Sabina Sheratska, née **Markowitz** (Basia's wartime
    companion)
Sala Grinzspan (Basia's school friend)
Sala Jacobowitz Reichmann (Leon Reichmann's first wife)

Preface

When you listen to a witness, you become a witness.
—Elie Wiesel (1928–2016)

It really was a dark and stormy night. My husband and I were sheltering from the rain at the bar at Nepenthe in Big Sur, California. The rain was so fierce that the place was empty, until two others came in and sat beside us. During the next couple of hours, Murray and I bonded with a woman named Helen West and her best friend, Marcia Greene, over wine and the free food sent forth from the kitchen, feeling cozy and protected from the raging storm. As we shared our stories, Helen's mention of being born in Munich opened our conversation to the tale of how her mother, Barbara Reichmann, had survived the Holocaust as a young woman in her twenties, always keeping one step ahead of the Nazis and evading capture. It was a tale of such courage, integrity, and smart choices, filled with odd twists, amazing coincidences, romance, and great losses that, despite my heavy sweater, I kept getting goose bumps.

The story captivated me for an additional reason. As a teacher of English as a Second Language to immigrant adults, I was often amazed and troubled by questions from some of my students after we read

Holocaust stories together. They would ask if those horrific things had actually happened. This wasn't ancient history. Many Holocaust survivors were still alive. How could my wonderful students, many of them refugees and survivors themselves, not know of the genocide of World War II? Perhaps a personal and unusual story like Barbara's, with the dramatic appeal of good literature, would make the tragedy of the Holocaust real to them.

"This needs to be a book!" I urged Helen.

"I agree," Helen said. "But I'm not about to do it. I'm busy enough with my psychotherapy practice. I write the occasional poem or personal essay or journal article, but I wouldn't know where to begin taking on a book and wouldn't have time if I did."

"I'll do it!" I blurted out.

"What a gift!" she said. "I'll run it by my mother."

After some initial reluctance, Barbara agreed to the proposal Helen and I presented to her: to share her life stories with me for a book. Helen and I would be partners, collaborating on every aspect. Barbara and Helen entrusted me with authorship of the main narrative, crafting a book out of Barbara's memories from earliest childhood up to immigrating to America. Helen would write a coda at the end giving her perspective on Barbara's life from that time on. Helen would also serve as guardian of Barbara's story, ensuring that the characters and events were faithfully rendered. Barbara would have the final say on everything.

A few months later I was on a plane from Los Angeles to Washington, DC.

Helen invited me to stay at her home, and each morning for five days, ninety-year-old Barbara Reichmann—"Basia" to her family and intimates from Europe—drove from her apartment to Helen's house to let me interview her. We sat around the kitchen table, tape recorder on my left, laptop in front of me, yummy food from Helen surrounding us, and we talked. Barbara—bright, elegant, charming—had the most incredible memory, going as far back as age two. She so graciously and warmly shared with me the most intimate details of her life: her joys and her deep pain. My questions brought forth memories, including not only a wealth of factual details, but also what she remembered thinking and feeling, from her happy early life growing up in Poland to the years leading up to and through the Holocaust.

Back in Los Angeles, excited and stimulated by Barbara's story, I immediately started writing, e-mailing, and calling Helen for more information and clarifications from Barbara. I incessantly went over my notes and re-listened to the tapes to be sure to capture Barbara's voice. What Barbara told me was so vivid, so alive, so in the moment. I didn't feel *I* had the right to tell *her* story; only she should tell it. So I chose to write in the first person, and in the present tense, to capture the immediacy of her experiences, and as often as possible, I used her exact words and turns of phrase.

Helen was invaluable, helping me research details, linking me with people involved in Holocaust studies and with survivors. Emotionally consumed by Barbara's story, I finished the first draft in three months and sent it to Helen.

Two months later I was again in Washington, DC, to go over the draft with Helen and Barbara. We sat around Barbara's dining room table, feasting on her chopped liver, stuffed cabbage, and freshly baked almond cookies (*mandelbrot*). Barbara was able to add even more information and correct my Polish spelling; she said she was pleased with the manuscript.

This book is the result of that collaboration. All the events, names, details, and perspectives in this book are Barbara's. In addition to my personal connection with Barbara, I relied on Helen's insights into her mother's character and those of the many others appearing in this book, keeping the voice and portrayals authentic and the story accurate. Where some of the dialogue or a few details necessary for the narrative flow have been invented, we tried to keep to a standard of depicting the essential truth, consistent with the nature of the characters described and the actual events.

What you are about to read is the story of a seemingly ordinary woman who was anything but ordinary: a freethinker, a sensitive soul, a defiant resister, a pacifist, a dreamer whose extraordinary survival can be traced back to traits of character evident from earliest childhood, as this story reveals.

CLAIMING MY PLACE

Becoming Basia

I'm running from death
Looking over my shoulder
Heading straight for Her arms
—Helen Reichmann West, "Ouroboros"

1942

At long last the train is pulling out of the station. I wonder how long I have been holding my breath.

Out of the corner of my eye I see Pan (Mr.) Dobranski sitting next to me. I know it's not possible that he can hear the pounding of my heart. Even so, I reassure myself that the clatter of the train's wheels masks the sound. I am lucky to have him as my traveling companion. His typical Polish looks will help camouflage me from being discovered as a Jew.

Fortunately, there are no Nazi soldiers on the train; at least not in our car, at least so far.

Looking out the window, I see the houses of Piotrków fade quickly behind me. I slow my breathing and try to relax. I have six hours before we get to Nowy Sącz. Six safe, quiet hours to empty myself of my past, my name, my identity.

Sura Gitla Gomolinska is no more. According to my forged *Kennkarte,* I am now Danuta Barbara Tanska.

Suddenly, I'm in a panic to make sure I have my new identity papers with my new name. Barely moving, I put my left hand in my coat pocket. I won't take the card out to look at it. That could raise suspicions. Just feeling it between my fingers will give me peace.

It's not there!

A wave of nausea washes over me. With no identification I could be killed.

Desperately, my fingers search the deep pocket.

It couldn't have fallen out. This can't be happening, not here, not now.

My head spins until I remember that I had put it in my right pocket, not my left. I reach into my coat with my other hand.

There it is.

Such relief. I feel the card with my fingertips. I see it so clearly in my mind: there is my photograph; there is my new name on the gray cardboard the Germans use to identify Poles, not the yellow cardboard designating "Jew." I am no longer a Jew to be deported and sent to the camps, or worse; now, officially, I am a Pole.

But the sudden relief mingles with anger at myself. How could I have been so stupid to put the only thing that stands between life and death loose in a pocket, even a deep one? I had carefully decided not to put it in my purse. Purses can be stolen. But a pocket! Pockets have holes; a skilled thief could grab the card without my knowing. What was I thinking? But then I remembered that mad rush to get out of the ghetto. How could I have been thinking clearly about anything? I should have stuffed it in my bra where I had put my money. As soon as I have some privacy, I will put it there.

I feel reassured now that I have settled on that plan. As the train rushes forward, I wonder what I should call myself. Danuta? It's so perfectly Polish but I don't like the harsh sound of it. Barbara is nice and common but so formal. Sura Gitla was always called Gucia; such a sweet-sounding nickname.

My fingers are caressing the *Kennkarte* in my pocket and suddenly I see it, I hear it.

Basia . . .

That's who I will be. It feels so warm and familiar. It's a good nickname for Barbara and it has the same sweet sound as Gucia.

I lean against the window and say goodbye to Gucia and my past. Basia is now journeying forward to the resort town of Nowy Sącz and her uncertain future.

First Grade

A desire for knowledge for its own sake, a love of justice that borders on fanaticism, and a striving for personal independence—these are the aspects of the Jewish people's tradition.
—Albert Einstein (1879–1955)

1922

Gucia, Gucia!" Krysia calls to me. "Gucia, wake up. Have you forgotten what day it is?"

Krysia has been our maid since I was an infant. It is because of her that I speak such fluent Polish. She throws off my quilt, and when she sees me lying there, she gasps, covers her mouth, and jumps back in surprise.

I leap out of the bed fully dressed, shaking with laughter.

"But Gucia, with shoes on, and in your bed?" She is horrified but can't stop herself from laughing along with me.

How can she think I would ever have forgotten this day? I have been awake since the Kosciul Bernardinski church bell struck three a.m. Then I had quietly dressed myself, being careful not to wake my ten-year-old sister, Hela, who was sleeping like a log next to me in the bed we share.

Today, as usual, when the sun peeped through the lace curtains at sunrise, Hela woke up and got dressed. I pretended to be sound asleep. She probably didn't remember what an important day it was for me and so she didn't try to wake me.

As I had lain there waiting for Krysia to come get me, my teeth chattered with excitement, little shivers going up and down my body. It is to be my first day of first grade . . . a day I have waited and yearned for as long as I can remember.

Krysia straightens my dress and unwinds my braids. She explains, as she often does, that my hair is just too fine to make good braids and that fine blond wavy hair is just as beautiful as thick straight hair. As usual, I don't believe her. She ties my wispy hair away from my face with a blue satin ribbon. Then she puts my pink knit cap on my head.

"Now, go see your mama and *tatte* (papa) and eat breakfast," she says.

I run out of the living room, where Hela and I sleep, and into the kitchen.

On this special September morning, Chana Chojnacka, our other maid, who is Jewish like us, is stirring the porridge at the stove. Two-year-old Josek—my middle brother—sits on the floor, banging the lids on some pots and pans and making a racket. Four-year-old Idek is eating toast with cranberry jam at the kitchen table. Hela is on her way to school, hugging Tatte goodbye, and Mama is nursing three-month-old Beniek.

She holds out her right arm to hug me, understanding my excitement. She smiles and says, *"Kum aher, Gitla, meine sheine meydle."* Come here, Gitla, my pretty little girl.

Mama always speaks Yiddish to me, but more and more I am speaking Polish to Krysia and my friends.

My mama is already elegantly dressed and ready to go to work. Soon she will leave the baby with Chana and walk the few blocks to Zamurowa Street to open our kosher butcher shop. Idek and Josek will stay home with Krysia, without me to play with them for the first time in their lives.

"It's my first day of real school, Mamashi," I say, hopping up and down in my brand-new black patent-leather Mary Janes. "Can I walk alone?"

The school is only one block away and I have been walking by myself to visit friends since I was very little. The streets are so safe. There are no strangers, no streetcars, only the occasional horse cart.

Mama smiles at me and says proudly, "Of course you may. You are such a big girl now."

I am excited to go all by myself, and I know that my parents can't take me anyway. They are much too busy. They both work very hard running the business and our apartment building, and there are so many of us to take care of when they come home.

The only time all of our family gathers together is for dinner each day at two p.m., except for Friday evening when we eat after Tatte comes home from *shul* (synagogue). Even then, our mouths share food but few words, apart from practical matters. Hela gabs about her friends and clothes and whatever she wants our parents to buy her. My little brothers Idek and Josek only talk nonsense and Beniek, the baby, just babbles.

I feel so different from all of them. I am burning with questions. There is so much I want to understand. I want to know why people have to die. What are other countries like? Why are some people kind and others cruel?

But though I am hungry for attention from my mama and *tatte*, I don't want to bother them with my questions and demands.

The answers, I know, are in books. When I was little, I thought people were just teasing me, pretending that the mysterious marks and squiggles in newspapers and the letters Tatte brought home from the post office really meant something. But now I have figured out that in school I will learn to read. A teacher will be there to explain everything and answer my questions. And then I will know the world!

Mama kisses me goodbye one more time and I leave the apartment. When I get outside, Rozia Nissenson, who lives in the apartment next to ours, and Sala Grinzspan, whose father owns the apartment building next door, run to catch up with me.

It is a crisp, almost-autumn day. The leaves on the linden trees are just beginning to turn yellow. Their fragrant white blossoms are drying up and falling like snow.

I am very proud of my beautiful new clothes—a navy blue pleated skirt and a matching blue top with a starched bright white sailor collar. My skirt and top are made of soft merino wool and Mama says the deep blue of the dress is very becoming to my amber-colored eyes. I am happy that it isn't too cold, so I don't have to hide my beautiful outfit under a bulky coat.

On my head I have a little pink cap that Bubbe Gomolinska—my father's mother—crocheted for me.

I have never worn my new shoes outside before, although I tried them on many times when Hela wasn't looking.

My only disappointment on this glorious day is that there are no heavy blond braids falling straight down my back.

I am glad I haven't eaten breakfast—just two sips of tea with milk and honey—because my stomach is quivering with excitement and dread.

Will the teacher like me? What if I am not a good student? Will I know any of the other students besides Rozia and Sala? Will I make any friends? Will I be the youngest? Will I be the shortest? Will it be as disappointing and as awful as the kindergarten I was forced to go to when I was four?

Finally, we get to the door of the beautiful brick school. Through the side gate I can see a lovely flower garden in the back. It is an extremely small school. There is only one classroom with the first, second, and third grades all together, but I know it is a prestigious private school for Jewish students from all over Piotrków Trybunal-ski, our town in central Poland.

Most of the students are already in the classroom, sitting in their newly assigned seats. There are two tables, each with a bench for two children, on one side of an aisle, and two tables and two benches on the other side. The tables and benches go back five rows. Most of the forty students are girls but there are some boys, too. The teacher is sitting behind her desk. It is on a small raised platform in front of a big blackboard. She is turned toward the door and holds a paper with all of our names.

My turn comes and my voice trembles a little as I announce, "Sura Gitla Gomolinska."

The teacher seems very nice. She is tall and thin and is wearing a gray dress with black dots. Her hair is light brown and she has it tied in a tight bun at the back of her head. She has small, round gold earrings dangling from her ears and a gold crucifix hanging from a chain around her neck. Her eyes are almost as gray as her dress.

She smiles at me and then she looks at the list. "Excuse me, could you say your name again slowly?" she asks gently.

I repeat my three names as clearly as I can and she looks at the list again.

"I am sorry, Sura Gitla, but I cannot find your name on the list. There is no record of your registration."

A feeling of horror comes over me, and for a moment I can't breathe. I realize, with my stomach sinking down to my shiny black Mary Janes, that my devoted father, who works so hard to take care of us, who never says no, and who would do anything to make us happy, has forgotten to register me for school.

I try to explain that my father has probably just overlooked this small detail of registration. My *tatte* has so many important things to worry about—our meat business and apartment building and large household.

The teacher says she understands. She expresses her regrets. "I am so sorry," she says, and she seems sincere. "You will just have to wait for next year, because we have absolutely no extra room, no room at all in the class. All the seats have been assigned. Come back next summer and have your father register you then."

And, as she gives me what seems like a death sentence, she smiles kindly and gently pats me on my head.

For the first time in my life I feel my heart break. It takes all my strength to hold back my tears as I somehow make my way home. As soon as I get there the tears burst out of me like a flood, racking my entire body with the sorrow and misery and helplessness I feel. And the anger and outrage at the injustice of it.

I want so badly to curl up in Mama's arms. Knowing I have to wait until she comes home at two o'clock is torture. I tear off my new clothes, put on an old smock, throw my favorite rubber ball in its net sling over my shoulder, and run out to the backyard to climb our old apple tree near the gazebo, my favorite private thinking spot.

I've had that rubber ball as long as I can remember. All the children I know have one. Mine is pink, green, and white, about the size of a soccer ball. We carry them in a crocheted sling over our shoulders (my sling is pink) and then, when we are ready to play, we each take out our ball and throw it against the walls and play games with each other. I know that I am not to take my ball to school. I am too old to play with a rubber ball there. But now it is comforting and, sitting in the apple tree, looking down at the gazebo, I keep slinging the ball in its strap against the branches of my old apple tree. I go over and over every painful detail of what has happened. And each time I start to cry again. I cling to the hope that Mama and Tatte will know how to fix this.

Finally, Mama comes home. I rush into her arms, sobbing, telling her my tragic story. She hugs me tightly and tries to calm me down. Soon Tatte comes home and Mama leads him to their bedroom to talk. When they come out, the look of pity I see on her face gives me a sick feeling.

"Bubbeleh," she says to me, "if the teacher says there are no more places for now, there is nothing we can do. Your *tatte* will register you to start school next year. When you start next year you will be one year older and smarter and able to be a much better student. I know you're disappointed now, but when you're grown up it won't even matter."

Not matter? How can she think that? What will I do for one whole year? With all my friends in school I'll have no one to play with. I turned six on May 15 of this year; next year I will be seven, and then I will be one year behind everyone else forever, always feeling stupid and ashamed.

The idea of just giving up makes me want to explode. I feel so alone. And I see clearly that I have to fight for myself.

Standing there before Mama and Tatte I make a decision and say, "I'm going back to school tomorrow to beg the teacher to let me in."

Tatte says, "No, you must not argue with the teacher. It would be disrespectful."

But Mama looks at me not with pity, but with pride. She turns to Tatte and says, "Itzak, let her go."

And as always, when it comes to the children, Tatte agrees with what Mama thinks.

So the next day, in my shiny Mary Jane shoes with my blue pleated skirt and blue sailor top and pink crocheted cap and wispy blond hair down my back, tied with a blue ribbon, I walk by myself to the school and present myself to the teacher.

The words burst out of me. "My name is Sura Gitla Gomolinska and I am here to learn. I cannot wait for another year. I cannot wait even for one more day. Please, please let me come to school."

The teacher gets a strange look on her face: displeasure, surprise, respect? She calmly shows me that there is no empty space on any bench, and how can I learn with no place to sit or write? She tells me that I cannot come to school. I must wait for next year. I am not registered and there is no place for me.

With tears in my eyes, again I walk slowly home and climb my apple tree.

"It is not fair. I want to learn. I will not give up," I say to the tree.

And so, I go back to school the next day, in my less-shiny Mary Jane shoes with my wrinkled blue pleated skirt and blue sailor top and pink crocheted cap and my thin hair down my back tied with a blue ribbon. And again I beg and again the teacher gently says no. But I do not give up. I return the next day and the next day and the next day and the next. Each time she says no and each day I go back. Week after week, every day but Saturday and Sunday, I go to school and plead with all my heart, fail in my efforts, and return the next day.

Do I just wear the teacher down? Does she feel pity for me after so many weeks of begging? Does she truly admire my perseverance, my stubbornness, my sense of justice, my deep, passionate desire for learning? I don't know. But one magical late-fall day, she finally gives in. She finds a little stool for me and places it in a corner of the room. After that, she allows my father to pay for the registration.

There is still no room, so I have to sit on the stool with my back to the blackboard, facing the other students, with no table to write on. I listen to everything the teacher says and try my best each day to learn as much as I can. The other students stare at me. My stubborn insistence to be admitted to school is unheard of. It would be too disrespectful for them to laugh or tease me openly, but I can feel their silent mockery as I sit at the front of the room, on that little stool, facing them. I feel like an outcast, though lucky to be there at all. Soon the staring stops.

Then one day in late November, the teacher comes to me and says, "Gucia, sometimes one person's misfortune is another's good luck. I have just learned that Voicek Pavinsky has polio and will not be coming back to school this year. There is a seat for you on the bench at the front table. Go sit."

I know I should feel bad for Voicek, but all I can feel is amazement that what I have given up even daring to hope for, to be a regular student with my own place like everyone else, has come to pass. I feel warm and glowing inside, triumphant. My standing up for myself has been rewarded. And just like that, my nightmare is over.

It is my first lesson in learning to think for myself and fight for what I believe is right—a lesson that will one day help give me the determination to fight for my life.

Piotrków Trybunalski

Ay, ay . . . the Yiddish print shops of Piotrków! They are known
throughout the world. In the Diaspora or in Israel, when a book,
a siddur, or a machzor is opened, the logo on the title page
is clear and distinct: "Printed in Piotrków."
—Elazar Prashker, "A Stroll Through Our Piotrków"

1922

My parents own a large apartment building at 21 Piłsudskiego Street
(proudly named after the Polish chief of state Józef Piłsudski), in the
middle of Piotrków Trybunalski, our small town southwest of Warsaw
and northeast of Kraków.

There are fourteen apartments in our three-story building, and we
have the largest, fanciest one. It runs the full length of the second floor
and has two lovely balconies facing the street. Ours, and three of the
other apartments on that floor, have private flush toilets inside them.
There is a big round porcelain box on the wall above our toilet, with a
chain hanging down.

When we pull the wooden handle of the chain to flush the toilet,
it makes an enormous whooshing sound. When I was a very little girl,
I was terrified of the monster who lived behind the toilet.

The tenants in most of the other apartments in the building have to make do with an outhouse that stands near the back of the courtyard behind our building, just inside the fence separating it from our huge, beautiful garden. Bolek, the janitor, keeps the outhouse spotless.

There is a bathhouse across the street where we go every two weeks, pay for a hot, steamy bath, and come home feeling fresh and squeaky clean.

On weekends, when farmers come in from the country to sell their fruits and vegetables, they park their wagons in our large cobblestone courtyard. At the north corner of the courtyard is a small shed where we keep our horse and wagon. Wojcek, the groom who cares for the horse, lives there, too. He has only one arm and I am afraid of him because of that.

On the south side of the courtyard are the four modest living quarters for the tenants who rent the four shops that face busy Piłsudskiego Street. Our garden on the other side of the fence has fruit trees, including my favorite apple tree and a lacy gazebo, and at the very back end of our property is a simple cottage rented by a poor, very nice Polish family, the Dobranskis.

In the back of the building there are a few rooms my parents use for storage and in the front, at street level, are four stores. There is the barber, Boris, a very nice man but not a typical Jew, because he keeps his shop open on Shabbos—the Jewish sabbath, which lasts from sundown on Fridays until sundown on Saturdays—so that the gentiles can get a shave and a haircut. I like walking past his shop because of the sweet smells of all his lotions and hair oils and soaps that waft outside.

Next to Boris is a dry cleaner and dyer named Pan Zarnowiecki. After his first wife died he married a very sweet, warmhearted woman who takes care of him and his son and the two more children they

GUCIA'S POLAND
1916 ~ SEPT. 1939

A.Elkington 2018

have together. Often, when I walk past their shop on my way to school, Pani (Mrs.) Zarnowiecka gives me delicious freshly baked *mandelbrot*.

Then there is Heska Szwartz, who owns the small grocery store and kosher catering business. Pan Szwartz is very ordinary. Shlomo Besser, the watchmaker, is not. He often beats his wife, even on Shabbos. She runs down Piłsudskiego Street screaming for help, with her husband running after her waving his belt, and the people on the street just laugh. Every time I see it happen I am outraged and angry. It is so cruel. People should go to her rescue, but no one ever does.

Our apartment is quite comfortable and inviting, furnished with the most stylish decorations and modern conveniences. My mother cares deeply about having a beautiful home for her family and my father cares deeply about pleasing my mother. We were the first in town to switch from the old flickering, smelly gaslights to the new, bright electrical chandeliers. Our walls are not painted like in the other homes but are covered in a shimmery green wallpaper with golden fleurs-de-lis. It looks like silk. Our furniture is beautiful, modern, and tasteful. My mother's favorite piece is their large wooden bed, because of the lovely landscape she had an artist paint on the headboard.

The kitchen is my favorite room in our apartment. It is always filled with such delicious smells, and there is the comforting warmth of the stove during those cold Polish winters and springs, the always-steaming teakettle, and the sturdy pine table where Chana and Krysia prepare our meals. We usually eat in the dining room, but the kitchen is the place for the babies to play on the floor and for me to find cookies and bread whenever I want.

Each evening at bedtime our two maids set up their two small sleeping cots against the west wall of the kitchen, and every morning fold them up and put them away. Because Chana is Jewish, my mother trusts only her to understand our kosher food laws.

Krysia, who is Polish, talks longingly of the delicious pork kielbasa and bacon she eats when she goes home to the countryside to visit her mother. Of course Mama would never allow such *traif* (non-kosher) foods to be brought into our home. And Krysia never eats with us at the table like Chana does. I don't know if that is her choice or my mother's.

At two in the afternoon every day but Friday, we all sit together as a family at the large, round, intricately carved mahogany dining room table for dinner. I love the scent and taste of Chana's fresh tomato soup with meat bones or the chicken soup with rice. In the winter we often have hot potato soup, or hot beef-and-cabbage borscht, and in the summer cold sorrel *schaav*, or leek-and-potato vichyssoise, or cold beet borscht with sour cream, a hard-boiled egg in the center, and a little dill sprinkled on top. When it is a meat day we have meatballs with potatoes and carrots or spinach, and sometimes veal cutlets or schnitzel, and Chana's scrumptious chopped liver with *schmaltz* (chicken fat). There are always fresh breads from the bakery on the corner at Jerozolimska Street: bialys, hard white rolls, rye bread, or pumpernickel. Of course every Shabbos we have our special freshly baked *challah* bread, deep yellow from the egg, beautifully braided, unlike my hair.

(Little do I suspect that years later, during the war, we would feel lucky finding any bread to eat at all, even bad-tasting, moldy, days-old bread! And how memories of delicious food would one day lift me out of my sadness, fear, and exhaustion during those long years.)

As the sun goes down on Friday night, we usher in the Shabbos, which is called welcoming the Shabbos Bride. The house is filled with such heavenly smells from all the special delicacies Chana has spent the day cooking. We gather around Mama as she lights the Shabbos candles and then covers her eyes and makes a blessing over them. With the candles casting a golden glow on her face and hair, Mama looks radiant. Then we sit at the dining room table for a feast. Often an *orech*, a stranger, someone my father has just met at the synagogue, will join us; maybe a poor man, maybe a traveler. It is a *mitzvah*, a good deed, to invite strangers for dinner on Shabbos.

We wait for Tatte to say the blessings over the wine and the *challah*, and then when my father is finished we all begin to eat. We start with *gefilte* fish, ground-carp dumplings. Out of respect for his special place of importance in our family, Tatte is served the head of the carp, the choicest delicacy saved just for him. Next comes chicken noodle soup. The noodles are always my favorite because I am fascinated by how much fun it is to make the dough for them. When Chana isn't too busy, she lets me help. After that, we eat the main course of roast chicken or goose with candied carrots and a butter lettuce salad with hard-boiled eggs and a sweet-and-sour vinegar-and-sugar dressing. After ending with a dessert of hot compote of apricots, prunes, and figs, we move into the living room, Tatte sitting in the special chair reserved for him alone.

On Saturday morning, Tatte goes to the synagogue, and when he returns at two o'clock we have our Shabbos dinner. Because we cannot light the oven for the twenty-five hours of Shabbos—using the oven is considered work and so is forbidden—this afternoon meal is mostly cold. We have *gefilte* fish and goose or chicken left over from Friday night, a cold meat aspic jellied from the front leg of a cow, and cold fruit compote. The main hot dish is the *cholent*, a delicious meat-and-barley stew. This is accompanied by a *kugel* of noodles or potatoes layered and baked separately, placed in the center of the table.

Each Friday, just before sundown, it is my job to take the pot of *cholent* and the pan of *kugel* that Chana has prepared to the Kalisher Bakery, a block away on Jerozolimska Street. Since the bakery ovens are already on, it is all right for the food to cook in the ovens on the Sabbath overnight. The next day, along with all of our neighbors, I pick up our own pots of steaming hot *kugel* and *cholent* for our Shabbos meal.

We are so full and happy that my family usually needs little else to eat until Sunday, but sometimes, on Saturday night, some of us go into the kitchen for a little cake and tea, but not all of us and not together. The food at our house is always plentiful, fresh, and delicious. But most of all on Shabbos.

Mama

A woman of valor who can find?
For her price is far above rubies.
The heart of her husband doth safely trust in her,
and he hath no lack of gain . . .
She looks well to the ways of her household,
and eats not the bread of idleness.
Her children rise up, and call her blessed;
her husband also, and he praises her.
—Proverbs 31:10–11, 27–28

1922–1924

Even though I had to beg and plead and fight to be admitted to first grade, or maybe because of that, from the very first day I have loved going to school, a real school. It is nothing like the kindergarten where my parents sent me when I was four, after Josek was born.

I hated it from the minute I walked in the door. I suppose they sent me there to distract me, because at that time there was turmoil in our home.

Soon after Josek's birth, Mama changed. I knew that something was different and not right. The apartment just wasn't the same. I had clear memories of my mother singing and smiling while she nursed Idek when I was two. Now a woman I'd never seen before came into the house to nurse Josek. Mama meantime had become wild in a way, walking up and down, up and down, mumbling and wringing her hands. Her once-sparkling eyes were glazed. When she looked at me, she seemed to look through me, as if she didn't see me at all. She didn't sing or laugh or hug me and she no longer brushed her beautiful golden hair one hundred strokes in the morning and one hundred strokes in the evening. Now when Mama went to open the butcher shop in the morning, she didn't seem to care about what she was wearing. Always before, she had been so stylishly dressed and had been extremely particular about her appearance. I was especially shocked to see my strong and loving mother scream at my father and say she hated him.

Unlike most Jewish couples, Mama and Tatte had not had an arranged marriage, a *shidduch,* but instead had met and fallen in love. Mama was smart and beautiful and lively and many young men had tried to win her. But she found all their showing off silly and instead was attracted to Tatte for his strong, calm, mature character and his dark good looks. They were always kind to each other, and though we could usually tell when there was trouble between them, they rarely argued in front of us.

Now she blamed all her unhappiness on Srul, the new employee who cut the meat at the butcher shop. From the first day since my parents had opened the store, Mama managed it, cut the meat for the customers, and took the money at the cash register, while Tatte had Wojcek drive him into the countryside to buy meat from the farmers and to help him load the horse cart. When Mama became pregnant with Josek, Tatte hired Srul out of concern for her health.

Mama wasn't so young anymore and she seemed more tired from this fifth pregnancy. Tatte saw how hard she worked—on her feet all day, lifting and cutting those heavy pieces of meat and running our household—and he knew she would cut her tongue out before she ever admitted anything was too much for her. So even though she told him she didn't need any help, he hired Srul against her wishes. Over the next few months of Mama's pregnancy, Srul got to acting like he was in charge, taking over and telling her what to do. She complained to Tatte that instead of a helper she had gotten a boss.

After she had Josek, it got worse. She came home angrier and angrier after spending all day in the shop with Srul. She said he was rude to the customers and disrespectful to her, and she begged my father to fire him. But Tatte said no. Tatte had an accommodating nature and had always admired Mama's ambition and gift for business, but on this he was accommodating to Srul at her expense and held firm.

Mama—suffering from what would one day be called postpartum depression—had become consumed by her hatred of their employee and her anger at my father. She felt Tatte didn't respect her judgment, and she was outraged at not being in control. She felt dishonored and helpless, and she broke.

I was frightened and bewildered that Mama had turned into such a stranger. And I was furious that I had to go to that stupid kindergarten every day. To me, that place was not a real school. It was just a silly waste of time—nothing but wild noisy little children running all over the place and playing meaningless games. The teacher was always screaming, and some of the children were not even toilet trained.

It was obvious that there would be no teaching or learning in this kindergarten. Since it was not a real school, I decided there was no reason to keep going. So, after about two months there, I simply got up one day and left. I came back home and because of the turmoil in our house, no one seemed to notice that I had stopped going to school. Chana and Krysia never mentioned that I wasn't in kindergarten. I guess they liked having me around.

After several months of this terrible chaos, Mama woke up one morning, washed and combed her luxuriant golden hair, and covered it with her beautiful custom-made *sheitel,* the wig Jewish women wore to cover their heads in public. (It was only in the privacy of our home that we could admire and brush Mama's wavy golden hair.)

Then Mama put on her nicest and newest tailored emerald-green dress and went to the stable and told Wojcek to ready the horse and wagon. She rode out to visit the Radoshitz Rebbe, who was famous for his healing powers (a rebbe is a rabbi who is considered especially important and holy). She told the rabbi of her troubles and complained about Srul. She said, "Rebbe, I have five children, four at home and little Chanusck in the cemetery. I have to be a mother to my children, but I am so very sick."

The Radoshitz Rebbe put his hands on Mama's head and said, "Go home, you will be a mother to your children, and you will be blessed with many more."

Overnight, Mama was Mama again. Tatte fired Srul the next day. Mama handed Josek to Chana as she walked out the door to open up the store. By herself, she cut all the meat and sold it. She was again my mama, a confident, beautiful, loving woman: a powerhouse and a real *mensch.*

Now, two years later, there is peace at home and I am in a real school. I finally have a place on the bench with the other students. My seat is in the front row and on the right side of the classroom, which is my good luck because I am deaf in my right ear.

Mama told me that when I was two, while she was out, I had been fascinated by a dust pile Chana made as she was sweeping the kitchen. We had no toys and I had to play with whatever was handy, and that dust pile apparently looked interesting to me.

When Chana went into the dining room, I started playing in the dust and found a small shiny brown coffee bean. I must have thought it was fun to put the bean in my ear, take it out, put it in, take it out, put it in, but then I couldn't get it out. It was stuck, and it hurt. I cried and Chana came running. She was so frightened. Mama wasn't home and Chana had to decide what to do.

She took me to a *feldsher*, a kind of healer, and when he tried to re-move the bean, by mistake he pushed it in even farther. When Chana brought me home to my mother, Chana was distraught over what had happened and how hard I was crying. She told Mama how sorry she was; she was only trying to save money by not going to a doctor. Of course Mama understood completely and wasn't angry with Chana. She was just upset for me.

Mama said that the *feldsher* was a quack and immediately took me to a real doctor in Piotrków, but *he* pushed the coffee bean in so far it punctured my eardrum.

After that my ear would often get infected and pus would ooze out. It must have been painful but I don't remember suffering from it. What I do remember is how happy it made me to get so much attention from Mama. She took me to many doctors, once even to Warsaw, the biggest city in the country, when I was three. We stayed with her cousin. I was excited to be in the capital, and I went outside by myself to go explor-ing. There was a huge commotion when I got back, as if I would have wandered off and never returned, and I felt so loved in that moment because of the attention. Over those years I blossomed because of all the special love and concern I received from my mother.

As I got older, I became self-conscious about my deafness and decided never to tell anyone about it.

In school, I am a sponge and absorb everything that we are taught and more. I am never without a book in my bag, in my bed, in the apple tree. After the triumph of finally being registered and then getting my own seat and place at the table, I am the happiest child in the world. I am sure that I will always be able to overcome any future obstacle.

But then only a week later, after getting my own seat on the bench, I learn that happiness doesn't last for long. On a snowy Thursday, Rozia's father asks me to walk with her to school the next day. She is always late and he thought if she walked with me she would be on time. I enjoy walking by myself, singing and daydreaming, but of course I say yes.

As usual Rozia is late coming out of her apartment, and on the next block she slips and falls in some slush. After we brush the wet snow off her clothes, she walks very slowly, complaining that her ankle hurts. By the time we get to school, we are both late and the teacher is angry and punishes us. She makes us stand in opposite corners in the front, with our backs to the blackboard, facing the class.

Rozia laughs, her dark eyes sparkling, her black curls dancing on her shoulders, while I break down in tears. It is Rozia's fault but I am the one who suffers. I am extremely embarrassed, humiliated, and angry. After all those difficult weeks of begging and pleading to be admitted to the school, and then being stared at as I sat on my little stool, I lose control and cry in front of my classmates. This makes me feel even more ashamed.

Later, sitting on a limb of my apple tree, I vow I will never let myself cry in front of people again.

After that terrible day I am never late again.

* * *

Over the rest of these first three years of grade school, I come to feel even more at home in school than with my own family. By the end of first grade, Beniek is toddling all over the house. Unlike those awful weeks after Josek was born, this time life at home doesn't change very much, except now Mama has even less time to pay attention to me. So all my attention goes to school. Maybe if I had gotten the sister I have been secretly wishing for, my life at home would have felt more interesting. Even at school, while I do well and get good grades, I never feel like I am anything special, just me, until a life-changing event at the end of the third grade.

We are having an arithmetic lesson and the teacher asks us, "If a Polish worker makes two hundred and ten new Polish *zlotys* per week, how many does he make each day?"

Many students quickly raise their hands to shout out, "Thirty *zlotys*!" But I say loudly, "No, the right answer is thirty-five *zlotys*."

The teacher says, "*Dobra*, Gucia! In my twenty years of teaching you are the first student to answer that question correctly! What a bright thinker you are!" And she turns to the class and says, "Learn to use your mind like Gucia. Figure things out. Polish workers don't work seven days a week, you know. On Sunday they go to church and rest. You should have divided by six and not seven!"

I am glowing. I feel for the first time a sense of being special and a confidence that I can trust myself to figure out what is true, what makes sense, and how to solve a problem even if no one else agrees.

Fourth Grade

Happy the pupil whose teacher approves his words.
—Jewish proverb

1925–1926

The new year starts out bittersweet for our family.

First, in January, our Jewish maid, Chana Chojnacka, gets married and moves away to Belgium. Although we are very happy for Chana, we are sad for ourselves. She has been our maid since before Hela was born and she is like family to us. In fact, Mama holds the wedding in our front parlor and pays for Pan Heska Szwartz to cater the dinner.

It is a very small wedding because Chana has no family in Piotrków, nor does her husband, Herschel. Papa and Uncle Josef are two of the four honor attendants who hold up the *chuppa*, the ritual canopy held over the bride and groom to represent the new home they will create. Then Chana walks around Herschel seven times, symbolizing the seven days of creation. The rabbi recites the marriage blessings over a silver cup of red wine, and then Chana and Herschel each drink from that cup. Herschel puts a simple gold wedding ring on the forefinger of Chana's right hand and recites his vows. My mama cries when the rabbi wraps his blue-and-white-striped prayer shawl, his *tallis,* around Chana and Herschel, as he pronounces them man and wife. Then Herschel crushes a glass wine goblet, wrapped in a white linen napkin, under his right foot, to remind us of the destruction of the Temple in Jerusalem and the sadness that we sometimes have in life, and then we all cry out, *"Mazel Tov!"* Congratulations!

Mama hugs Chana awkwardly, because Mama is very pregnant. Again!

In February, soon after Chana and Herschel leave, Mama has her seventh baby and I am happy that it is a little girl. Now at last I will have a sister I can play with. My other sister, Hela, is four years older than I and we have always been worlds apart. All we have in common is that we have shared the same bed since I was a baby. Hela is so stylish, with a taste for fine things, and she feels free to ask for whatever she wants.

Mama, who is generous by nature and especially with us, never says no to her children. I've heard some grownups say we are spoiled, so I deny myself things to prove them wrong. Mama is always wanting to buy me my own new clothes, but I would feel selfish to let her waste money like that when the clothes Hela has outgrown are so beautiful and still look good as new. So I find an inexpensive seamstress in the neighborhood, not like the expensive one who comes to our house, and she alters Hela's hand-me-downs to fit like they were made for me! Even though I was saving her money, I think Mama was a little disappointed because she has fun dressing us up. But when she told me how proud she was that I am so resourceful, I felt a secret glow inside that gave me so much more pleasure than I ever could have gotten from a new dress.

And now I have a little sister, someone I can cuddle and take care of and play with. They name her Rifka after my father's mother, who has just died. My little sister is very cute. She has Mama's beautiful green eyes and little wisps of strawberry-blond hair, like Hela. Mama lets me hold her as a reward when I finish all my homework early.

But then comes a shocking tragedy. Three months after Rifka is born, the new Polish maid, Anya, lets Rifka roll off the table as she is changing her diaper, and my little baby sister is dead.

The grief I feel is overwhelming. Everyone is devastated. Following our Jewish tradition, the day after little Rifka dies, we bury her in the Jewish cemetery in a plain pine box, next to Chanusck, the sister I never knew, who got sick and died a year after I was born, when she was three. All I am aware of are the prescribed rituals called *shiva* that get us through that first week of mourning. It is comforting having those procedures to follow when we are too numb to think. Uncle Josef, Mama's favorite brother, and Tanta Sura come right over. They cover all the mirrors and windows in the house with white cloths. The religious reason for this is to remind us that death is a time to contemplate the deep mysteries of life and not be distracted by vanity. The superstitious reason is that the Angel of Death is so ugly that if he sees himself in the mirror when he comes into the house he will get angry and take someone else, too.

Throughout that week of sitting *shiva,* those of us in mourning sit on low wooden stools as friends come to visit and comfort us in our grief. And each day a *minyan* of ten men, including Uncle Josef and Rozia's and Sala's fathers, come to say prayers. Tatte says the Kaddish, the mourners' prayer.

Going back to school, to my other life, gives me comfort in the face of this tragedy.

In September, I enter the fourth grade at a public school called Maria Konopricka. It is so convenient for me. The city had rented the ground floor of the apartment building next to mine, the one that Sala

Grinzspan's father owns and where they live. This is where the school is, so close that even Rozia won't be late for classes.

My school days all seem to run into each other. We have to memorize, memorize, memorize, and so often I am bored. But one big event stands out.

Sometimes a teacher will choose a favorite student to carry her books to school. It is always considered a great honor. It is near my birthday in May when my teacher, Pani Grabowska, asks me to come to her house to carry her books. I think I will fall off my chair I am so struck with shock and pride.

She gives me the directions to her house on the outskirts of the city. I get up two hours earlier than usual because I know it will take almost an hour to walk there and another hour back to school. Fortunately it is May and not cold and the blossoming trees and flowers, the cheerful songs of the birds, make me very happy along the way.

Pani Grabowska meets me at her front door and when she goes to get the books, I peek inside. All I can see is the large front room but I take everything in immediately. Instead of fancy gold-embossed wallpaper and shellacked wooden floors painted a shiny cinnamon color, like at our house, she has plain white walls and a dark wood floor with a small Oriental carpet in the middle. Unlike our heavy mahogany furniture, she has lots of wicker furniture painted a nice shade of forest green. There is a comfortable armchair, a rocking chair, a round table with glass on the top, and a big curvy couch. On the seats and backs of all the furniture are matching light green fluffy pillows, embroidered with large red and pink roses. On the sparkling glass top of the round table is a simply framed photograph of a handsome young blond man in a Polish soldier's uniform. Lying next to the photo is a single red rose and a small glass jar with a lighted religious candle. I remember hearing that Pani Grabowska had a boyfriend who was killed during

World War I. It all seems very romantic to me. Although she lives on the outskirts of the city in a little cottage, I think her house is much more beautiful and elegant than mine.

I take the heavy bag of books and practically fly to the school. For the rest of the week I carry those books back and forth. Pani Grabowska walks by herself and arrives at the school a little later than I do.

In 1926 Mama is pregnant again, and now that I am ten I feel differently than when I was eight. When Rifka was born, I had been so excited. Now, at ten, I feel embarrassed that my mama is having another baby and a little afraid that the new baby will die, too. When Regina is born, she looks just like Rifka, with large bright green eyes, but with curly red hair. She is a strong baby and the new maid, Janova, loves and watches her very carefully. While there would always be sorrow over losing Rifka, Regina brings the joy of new life back into our home.

Judaism

In lighting the Sabbath candles, women help take away some of the darkness of the world.
—Hendla Libeskind Gomolinska

1926

I have always lived on a Jewish street in a Jewish neighborhood, sheltered and protected. My elementary school teachers and Krysia are the only gentiles I have ever known well, and I feel great love from all of them.

However, we do have one gentile tenant in our apartment building. He gets drunk and knocks loudly on our door, shouting that we are Christ killers. He threatens us, and we are all afraid, even Tatte. I don't understand why, but I know that he can make trouble for us just because he is a gentile and we are Jews. But these outbursts are rare.

We are not a strictly observant family, but my mother has a deep faith. I was told that after my parents' marriage, their first Friday night together was the occasion of their first fight. My father had decided that as the man of the house he was free to establish his own family traditions and no longer needed to blindly follow the practices of his father. After working hard all week, he preferred spending a quiet evening at home with his new wife rather than attending synagogue. To my mother, this was unthinkable. It was all right for women and children to stay home, but she expected Tatte, like all good Jewish men over the age of thirteen, would go to synagogue and not dishonor his new family this way. After arguing and being unable to sway him, she walked out and went home to her mother. Her mother sent her right back, but Mama had made her point, and from that time forward, Tatte went to the synagogue every Friday night and never forgot to put on a *yarmulke* when he came back to make the blessings over the wine and *challah* for Shabbos dinner.

Aside from Tatte, none of us go to synagogue, except on the High Holidays: our New Year, Rosh Hashanah, and our Day of Atonement, Yom Kippur. But welcoming in the Shabbos is a special time for all our family every Friday night. At eighteen minutes before sunset, Mama puts a lace cap on her head. Her hands make three circles over the lit white candles standing tall in the two large silver candlesticks passed down from my great-grandmother.

Mama's beautiful blond head is bowed, her eyes closed, as she blesses God, who has given us His laws and commanded us to light the Shabbos candles. She sometimes says that maybe these little lights will take away some of the darkness of the world. She tells Hela and me that it is our responsibility as Jewish girls to always fight the darkness. Then Tatte says his blessings. The "religious" part is over, and we get to eat.

Like most of the Jews in Piotrków, we keep kosher. The laws passed down from God to Moses taught that "the kid should not be cooked in its mother's milk" and from that Jewish law and tradition it became forbidden to mix any meat products with any dairy products. If we cannot mix meat and milk (*fleishik* and *milchik*), then we must have different dishes and silverware and pots and pans for each of those categories. And then what do you do when you wash the dishes? Krysia is very careful to use only the red-striped dishcloths to wash and dry the meat dishes and the blue-striped for the dairy. Even the soaps are striped, one red and one blue so that the suds from one set could never accidentally contaminate the other.

But this is nothing compared to what has to be done for Pesach (Passover). In preparation for this holiday, our maids work very hard to clean all traces of any of the forbidden leavened foods, the *chummetz*, out of the house. They go through all the drawers looking for crumbs and sweep all the corners of the apartment with extra care. It is not enough to simply throw away what they have collected with the regular trash; all of it has to be burned on the morning before the holiday begins. Then they put all the everyday dishes and silverware and pots and pans and towels and soaps in storage and take out two other (one for the meat and one for the milk) special Passover sets of plates and silverware and pots and pans and towels and soaps, just for the eight days to celebrate the holiday of Pesach. And once Pesach is over, everything is switched around again.

This is standard Jewish observance in Piotrków, even for more secular Jews like us. But when I am around nine years old, I start to wonder why at home we pick and choose, following some of the laws and not others. I'm not used to following rules that don't make sense to me. Mama always explained why I should or shouldn't do something, but mostly let me decide what to do for myself. So if we can decide which laws to follow, why obey any of the ones that don't make sense? But if we're supposed to let God decide, shouldn't we obey them all? I am still best friends with Rozia and Sala, but I start spending more time with Itka Ber, who lives one building over and whose family is strictly observant.

They are very devout and very poor. Pani Ber does all the work in their small shop, which is on the ground floor of their building. She bakes *challah* and makes ice cream, and that is just about all they sell in their store. Pani Ber is so sweet! In the summers, when Itka and I are playing at my house on our balcony one flight above the street, her mother comes outside with a bucket attached to a rope. She puts a dish of ice cream in the bucket, throws the other end of the rope up to us, and Itka and I loop it to the balcony railing. Then we pull on the rope to raise the bucket and sit on my balcony eating ice cream and watching all the people walking up and down Piłsudskiego Street.

Meanwhile, Pan Ber does not have a job to provide for his family because he spends every day at the synagogue praying and studying the Talmud. This is the rabbinical commentary interpreting all the laws in the five books of our Torah, given to us by God. The men debate the tiniest legal intricacies, even though a lot of the situations they ponder don't even exist anymore in the modern world. For the very religious Jews, this study is the highest calling and what our most brilliant rabbinical scholars devoted their lives to. I used to think this was a silly waste of time, but now from school and talking to Itka, I'm learning why this is important.

We're not born smart enough to comprehend the ways of God. But He did make us smart enough to figure out how to be good Jews. God wants us to be just, fair, and merciful with one another and to care for ourselves and to revere Him. So we follow God's laws because He knows what's good for us, whether we understand or not. Deciding how to apply them throughout changing times is the part we Jews, relying on our Talmudic scholars, use our intelligence to figure out for ourselves. That's why it's okay for the men to spend the day thinking and arguing and studying and praying without making any money while their wives work to support their families.

I understand the explanation for this arrangement, but I'm not sure how I feel about it.

Every Friday night my family has a delicious Shabbos dinner, but the Bers have a Shabbos festival! They eat and sing and pray. Unlike my family, the Bers keep Shabbos inside the house, too, not just outside. Itka tells me that Shabbos is our holiest day, even more than Rosh Hashanah and Yom Kippur. God gave us Shabbos so that no matter what hardships or pain we might be suffering, this one day a week we feel joy and thank God for the gift of life. Even when we are in mourning and sit *shiva* for a week, on Shabbos we are not supposed to grieve. And if we have to choose between going to a wedding or a funeral of people equally close to us, we go to the wedding. The gift of life is more important than the pain of death.

In Genesis, the first book of the Torah, we learn how God created the world in six days and then on the seventh He rested; so we are forbidden from working and must also take this day, our Shabbos, to rest, study Torah, and forget all worldly concerns. But what counts as work? The Torah gives us thirty-nine categories of work based on the tasks of agriculture, like planting and plowing and harvesting and engaging in commerce. This is from olden times when all of our ancestors provided for themselves by farming the land. Since farmers aren't allowed to harvest their crops on the Sabbath, the rabbis taught that we must refrain from any similar act, like pulling a blade of grass from the earth or picking a leaf off the branch of a tree. And to protect us from accidentally breaking this rule, we are forbidden from climbing a tree.

On Shabbos, the Bers don't buy anything, nor carry any money. They can't even push Itka's little baby brother in his baby carriage. They don't light any fires, cook any food, turn on their gas lights, take a train, or write. If they had a radio or telephone, they wouldn't be able to use them. It is also forbidden to cut or tear anything, so just before Shabbos, Pani Ber rips a lot of toilet paper into little pieces and stacks them into piles to use during the Shabbos. (The rule I find so funny is that because writing business records and contracts means making marks, we are forbidden from peeing in the snow!) I am intrigued by all of this.

Itka also teaches me that God wanted Moses to lead our people away from the barbaric practices of the other tribes. Five thousand years ago, some of them would sacrifice an animal and then drink its warm blood as it was dying. I shiver when she whispers that some of those tribes would even drink the blood of the enemies they had killed, so they could gain the dead men's power. Itka says God wanted to be sure that we Jews never practiced animal cruelty or human sacrifice, so He told Moses to proclaim that none of the meat we eat should have blood in it. Also, we had to be sure that the animal had been killed mercifully. The other tribes would keep hitting the poor animal over the head, and it would die slowly and painfully. So instead we cut the jugular vein in the throat so that death comes quickly and a lot of the blood leaves the animal's body. It's also why we can never eat meat from the rump or back legs of the animal, where the large veins might still have blood in them. This is one of those times when the law makes sense to me.

Then some of the other laws of *kashruth*—the kosher laws—don't make sense. We are allowed to eat only the meat of an animal that both chews its cud and has a cloven hoof, like a cow, a sheep, a goat, or a deer. Animals with only cloven hooves, like the pig or rabbit, or that only chew the cud, like a camel, are forbidden. Only fish that have both fins and scales are kosher; shellfish like shrimp and oysters are not.

But we are to obey them all. I never thought about what Mama and Tatte did in the shop as anything besides a business to make money for us. But now I see what an important responsibility this is, making sure that all the customers are correctly obeying God's laws.

One time when I sleep over at Itka's house, we wake up early in the morning to get ready for school. Pan Ber has the flu and is too weak to go to the synagogue to pray. Pan Ber normally prays three times every day at the synagogue, and even though he is feeling sick, he has still gotten out of bed at dawn to pray at home. He is standing in the sun parlor, facing east and praying very softly, bowing his head and moving his body up and down in a lovely rhythm. This is called *davening*. I've seen the men praying like this when I go to *shul* on the High Holidays, but I didn't know you could do it by yourself at home. On the inside of his left arm, just above the elbow, there is a little black leather box held in place by a black leather strap wrapped seven times around his arm and three times around his middle finger. Another box rests on the center of his forehead, with its leather strap hanging down over his right shoulder. I learn that these are called *tefillin* (also *phylacteries*). He also wears a *tallis*, the white prayer shawl with blue stripes, wrapped around his head and shoulders. I am practically hypnotized watching Pan Ber pray and I feel bereft that my father is not a "real Jew."

Itka already knows most of the 613 *mitzvot* (commandments) from the Mishnah, the oral law handed down over the generations and put in writing by Maimonides in the twelfth century. She says that 248 are positive "Thou shalts" and 365 are negative "Thou shalt nots." I decide to try and learn all 613 *mitzvot* myself. Then I will know what is the right thing to do every minute of my life.

I suppose I want something more to believe in, some kind of focus. I yearn for some religious standards, some rules of what is wrong or right.

For one year I strictly and wholeheartedly keep all the laws and commandments Itka Ber teaches me. My sister and brothers make fun of me but I don't care. My religious discipline gives me comfort and quiets all the noisy questions that have always bubbled in my mind. I feel safe and calm, and at peace with myself and my world.

And then my views change. Is it because I get older and more practical, more questioning; or is it only because of what Itka does to me at school?

It is in late September, just before the Jewish New Year. In our home economics class the teacher, Pani Lewinova, holds a contest to see which student can sew the most perfect hem of an apron. Itka's comes out puckered. I love the waviness of it and think it looks beautiful and tell her so. The teacher has other ideas and judges that my boring, straight hem is the winner. Itka gets very angry with me. Her dark eyes bore through me and she says that I lied to her about her "beautiful hem" just so I could win. She says I am not a good friend and she should have won the contest. She pouts and won't talk to me.

But then, at the beginning of Rosh Hashanah, Itka starts acting like we are friends again, because at this holy time of year we are meant to let go of any hard feelings toward other people. But her friendship only lasts for the ten holy days from Rosh Hashanah to Yom Kippur, when Itka again stops talking to me.

I am really hurt and shocked by this selfish behavior from my dear friend. How can I be friends with someone who doesn't wish me well and falsely accuses me of tricking her and lying? And how can she be so hypocritical and think that following the rules but not the meaning and spirit behind them is the point of being religious? She may know all 613 *mitzvot*, but that by itself doesn't make her a good Jew.

Maybe it just isn't in my nature to obey without doubting, but gradually I become more and more skeptical. So much of what might have made sense when Moses took the Israelites out of Egypt five thousand years ago doesn't seem to me to apply to life in the twentieth century.

If the Sabbath is a day of rest, why do the Bers have to work so hard not to work?

Why can't they push the baby in the carriage on Shabbos? They have to carry him instead and he is very fat.

If anything, Pani Ber, who strictly keeps Shabbos, works harder than women like my mama, who don't.

I realize I don't have the faith to make my religious practice feel like more than just shallow rituals. And without true belief and sincere devotion, it makes no sense to keep it up. I still yearn for deeper meaning and purpose in my life, but I feel I'll have to find another way, one that is true to the values I believe in but is not tied to religious practice or even to belief in God.

Zionism

Palestine is our unforgettable historic homeland . . .
The Jews who will it shall achieve their State . . . whatever
we attempt there for our own benefit will redound mightily
and beneficially to the good of all mankind.
—Theodor Herzl (1860–1904)

1928

Somewhere, from my very first memories, I have always understood that a Jew must work for *tikkun olam*: healing the world. We are the chosen people, chosen to improve the world, to work toward world peace and justice for all.

Searching for a purpose, a cause to believe in, I am attracted to Zionism. There are many branches of Zionism based on different principles and political philosophies from far left to far right, some atheistic and some very religious, but all devoted to establishing a Jewish state, Eretz Yisrael, in our ancestral homeland of Palestine. Together with Sala and Rozia, I join Hanoar Hatzioni. Our movement is not religious or political but devoted to educating young people about Jewish culture and preparing them to immigrate to Eretz Yisrael.

We meet in an apartment we call "the clubhouse" once or twice a week, after school and homework are finished. Leaders come and talk to us about the land of Israel and Zionism and teach us Israeli songs and dances. In the summers we go to camps and learn to swim and develop other practical skills for taking care of ourselves outdoors. We are like all the youth scouting organizations in different parts of the world, but with the extra passion of our cause.

Even though Zionism has been around since the early 1900s, frightening trends in Poland and throughout Europe since the end of World War I make my devotion to Zionism feel especially urgent. The Versailles Treaty ending that war in 1918 punished the defeated Germany harshly. The German economy has been getting worse and worse, with life extremely hard, jobs and food scarce, and the Germans feeling humiliated and demoralized. At this difficult time, a new political movement called Fascism is attracting followers. Fascism offers a utopian vision of honor and power and superiority. It is also a way to place the blame for hardship on others, and the Jews are the easiest target because anti-Semitism has a long history in Europe.

Fortunately, except for my fear of our gentile tenant, I have never personally experienced anti-Semitism. We Jews all live safely together in our Jewish communities, and my parents don't talk about it much. But I know about the suffering inflicted on Jews in the past from my history and Torah studies in school. Now we are hearing horrible stories of recent pogroms (massacres of Jews and destruction of their villages), hatred, and discrimination against Jews—which, all too soon, we will experience firsthand.

Even though the New Testament teaches that Jesus had been a rabbi and that Mary and Joseph and the twelve disciples were Jewish, for centuries the Church's teachings had encouraged prejudice against the Jews. It was said that Jews had killed Jesus and were the cause of many of the troubles in the world. Even in modern times some people still believe that on the days before Passover, Jews kill Christian children to use their blood for baking the *matzot* (unleavened bread) we eat during the Seder, the feast that begins the eight-day celebration of Passover. They have even said Jews would put the blood of those murdered children in their wineglasses to drink.

At the Seder we always set an extra glass of wine along with an empty plate and chair for the prophet Elijah. Since he still hadn't arrived by the time we were finished eating, we cleared the table but moved his cup of wine to the center and left the front door open for him. Some of the wine evaporated overnight, and the next morning, seeing that the level of the wine was lower in the glass, we children believed that Elijah had actually come.

Many years later, to my horror, I learned the real reason for the tradition of opening the door for Elijah, which had started in Europe in the Middle Ages. During the Seder, Jews would leave their front doors wide open so that, without needing to break down the doors, gentiles could easily see that Elijah's cup on the table was actually filled with wine and not with Christian blood. How can you explain to a child that some gentiles believed Jews would kill Christian children and drink their blood? So parents made up a tale about opening the door for the prophet so he could drink his glass of wine.

In Leviticus, the Torah says, "And Aaron shall place lots upon two goats: one 'For the Lord,' and one 'For Azazel, the fallen angel of the wilderness.' " We are told that in the time when the Temple still stood, on the Day of Atonement, the goat for Azazel would be given all the sins of the Israelites and sent into the desert, never to be seen again.

This was not just a tradition of the Jews. Throughout history, in religious celebrations, people of different faiths would symbolically put all their sins and troubles on a goat and send it into the desert or push it over a cliff. It was called the "scapegoat," and was a convenient way to get rid of things that frightened and troubled you. For over two thousand years Jews have been used by other cultures as scapegoats, especially once we were exiled from the Land of Israel and dispersed throughout the world. We have been blamed for any and every catastrophe, from the Black Death of the fourteenth century to droughts and pestilence and the economic downturns of the present. Time and time again Jews have been accused of poisoning wells and killing little children. Over and over, Jews were persecuted—beaten, tortured, murdered, and thrown out of their villages and adopted countries. How easy it has always been to blame the Jews—the new goats—for all sorts of problems.

Anti-Semitism is so easy to foment. Humans all fear the Other. Is it because we Jews keep together in our neighborhoods, and often speak our own language? Because we eat different food, because we dress differently, because we work so hard and are so successful? I don't understand why we are so suspected, so despised, but I know we are.

Now, in the 1920s, many of the Jews in Germany and Poland and Eastern Europe like my family and neighbors are hardworking, successful middle-class merchants and educated professionals in the few careers that are open to Jews, like teaching, engineering, and law. There are still certain restrictions. Becoming a government worker is not an option in many places. Nonetheless we live in civilized times. I had thought the horror stories of the pogroms belonged to history or to the Old Testament. But I start hearing of the virulent anti-Semitism growing in Fascist Germany. I am getting scared.

As Fascism flourishes in Germany, so Communism grows in Russia. Even before the Russians overthrew their czar in 1917, the Communist doctrine promised to eliminate all sense of class in society; they wanted all people to become economically equal. Yet although two of the founders of Communism, Karl Marx (from Prussia) and Leon Trotsky (born Lev Davidovich Bronstein, from Ukraine), were Jews, the Russians, and especially the Ukrainians, ignore that fact, and like the Fascists, are stirring up anti-Semitism, using the Jews as scapegoats.

We know from our history classes that this hatred is not new. In the nineteenth century the Russians and the Ukrainians and the Cossacks and the Poles had used the Jews as scapegoats in the countless bloody pogroms in their countries. Then Jews were blamed for the starvation and misery after World War I. And so nothing has really changed. It is always "Blame the Jews." The only thing that changes now and then is what we're being blamed for.

In the face of all this, small groups of young Jews have banded together to try to make the world a better place. The first step, we believe, is to end our two-thousand-year exile and reestablish the Jewish homeland in what is now called Palestine, an area that fell under British rule after World War I. Our Zionist movement is about Jewish culture more than the Jewish religion. It is about having a place where our heritage will not make us scapegoats or targets of discrimination. We want a place where we can live as ordinary people, a nation like every other; not just merchants or bankers or lawyers or intellectuals, but also farmers and doctors and plumbers and thieves. Normal! We are certain that our new Zionist society, based on freedom, equality, and justice, will allow man's highest nature to flourish. We will be a model to all the nations and anti-Semitism and discrimination will disappear from the earth. How idealistic we are; how fervent in our beliefs. We never doubt that we can change the world!

At the time that I join Hanoar Hatzioni, I read a book about Theodor Herzl, a major figure in modern Jewish history. Herzl was born in Budapest, Hungary, in 1860, and was educated in Vienna, Austria. It was there that he first experienced anti-Semitism and started writing articles and plays trying to figure out a solution to that centuries-old problem of hatred of and prejudice toward the Jews. He moved to Paris in 1894 and worked as a journalist. He was appalled by the trial of the French captain Alfred Dreyfus. Dreyfus had been falsely accused of treason. Everyone knew that Dreyfus had been framed just because he was Jewish. Herzl heard mobs of people screaming "Death to the Jews." He was particularly shocked because the French took such pride in adhering to the principles of the Enlightenment and rational thought. They even fought their famous French Revolution to create a society based on liberty, equality, and fraternity! Herzl came to believe that only if the Jews had their own country could they prevail in their battle against the evils of anti-Semitism.

In 1896 he wrote a book called *The Jewish State*. He proposed that Jews raise money to buy back the land of Palestine, their ancestral home, and end their two-thousand-year exile. Herzl said we needed to return to Zion and named his movement Zionism. I am so moved when I read his book that I copy his words into my journal:

> We are a people—one people.
>
> We have sincerely tried everywhere to merge with the national communities in which we live, seeking only to preserve the faith of our fathers. It is not permitted us. In vain are we loyal patriots, sometimes super-loyal; in vain do we make the same sacrifices of life and property as our fellow citizens; in vain do we strive to enhance the fame of our native lands in the arts and sciences, or her wealth by trade and commerce. In our native lands where we have lived for centuries we are still decried as aliens, often by men whose ancestors had not yet come at a time when Jewish sighs had long been heard in the country.

Oppression and persecution cannot exterminate us. No nation on earth has endured such struggles and sufferings as we have. Jew-baiting has merely winnowed out our weaklings; the strong among us defiantly return to their own whenever persecution breaks out . . . Wherever we remain politically secure for any length of time, we assimilate. I think this is not praiseworthy . . . Palestine is our unforgettable historic homeland . . . Let me repeat once more my opening words: The Jews who will it shall achieve their State. We shall live at last as free men on our own soil, and in our own homes peacefully die. The world will be liberated by our freedom, enriched by our wealth, magnified by our greatness. And whatever we attempt there for our own benefit will redound mightily and beneficially to the good of all mankind.

I am fired up by these ideas and principles with a passion I've never felt before, and so I become an ardent Zionist.

The Gymnasium

He who studies cannot follow a commercial life: neither can the
merchant devote his time to study.
—Talmud

1927–1934

Graduating from Maria Konopricka at the end of fifth grade in 1927 is the beginning of our future lives. A few students simply find jobs; those of us who want to continue our education can either learn a trade in the Jewish vocational school or enroll in the Jewish Gymnasium for an academic course of study. Poles and Jews have separate Gymnasiums, and we all have to pay tuition, as free public education in Poland ends after fifth grade. So that is what I do. I attend the Stowarzyszenie Zydow-skich Szkol Srednich (Jewish Association Middle School) in Piotrków.

Nothing has really changed since my father forgot to register me in first grade. Each month I need to remind my parents to pay my school fees. They are happy and proud to do this but too distracted by all their other responsibilities to remember on their own. The Gymnasium is an excellent school and it is considered an honor and a privilege to attend it. It is very convenient, only a fifteen-minute walk from home.

I love my classes there, even though we attend six days a week (only off on Shabbos), and the work is extremely demanding. We are given hours of homework every night. But it is so stimulating and exciting that I look forward to school every day. We have classes in math, physics, geography, and history, especially the history of Poland. We study Latin, German, and Hebrew, as well as Polish literature and Greek mythology. The girls have to learn home economics, plus we have gym. My favorite course is Latin. The teacher, Pan Wajsinger, is young and handsome. All of us girls are in love with him. (I sometimes wake up in the middle of the night conjugating Latin verbs, realizing that I have been dreaming of him.)

Pan Wajsinger and I have started off on the wrong foot. The first week I was in his class, we were taking our first test. I had written all my answers on a scratch paper and was re-copying them neatly onto the test when the time was up. I was sitting in the first row on the farthest right (because of my ear), so he picked up my test paper first. But I hadn't finished copying it. I grabbed it out of his hands and he took it back from me. That seemed so unfair and before I could stop myself, I blurted out, *"Swinswo"* (piggish). I thought I would die of embarrassment. Pan Wajsinger didn't call on me for many weeks, and I suffered. But then he let it go, and I think he enjoyed having me as his student.

In 1931 Pan Wajsinger, an ardent Zionist, decides to emigrate to Israel, and Latin is never the same after that.

Each day of school begins with two hours of Hebrew classes. The first hour we read the Old Testament, and while we study the Holy Scriptures the boys have to put on their *yarmulkes* to cover their heads. The second hour we learn Sephardic Hebrew, the language spoken in Israel.

Most of the time, Pan Rosenblum makes us just memorize, memorize, memorize, and the minute he asks a question we have to answer it, automatically and without thinking, like machines. We have hours of homework to memorize as well. This makes me very angry, because I know that memorizing is not learning. There is no thought involved. I want to understand new ideas. I really dislike him intensely and can't bear to look him in the face.

One day he asks me, "Are you a Hasid's daughter, Gucia? Is that why you won't look at me?"

Of course he knows who my father is and that we aren't Orthodox. I know that he likes me and that makes me terribly uncomfortable.

I feel disgusted by his question, look down to the floor, and say a loud, "No!"

Pan Rosenblum asking such a personal question and forcing us to work like slaves at memorization aggravates me so much that I organize a class strike. The next day, just before Hebrew classes start, we deliver a note to the principal explaining our protest and then all leave the school and go to the park for two hours. The day after the strike, Pan Rosenblum doesn't say a word about it; no one says anything. I don't think he ever suspected that I was the organizer of the strike. But from then on the memorization is much less.

We know from the minute we enter the Gymnasium that in order to matriculate we will have to pass the very difficult Matura, the final examination needed to go on to the university. Until recent years, students in both the Polish and Jewish Gymnasiums were tested for the Matura by teachers from their own schools, who had taught them what they would need to know in preparation for the test. But now the Polish government no longer officially recognizes the Jewish Gymnasiums and decrees that teachers from a Polish Gymnasium will come to our schools to test us for the Matura. This means we can be tested on anything, whether it's on our curriculum or not. We all know that the obvious purpose of this policy is to make the test so hard that few of us will pass. It's their way of keeping us out of the university without having official quotas.

Preparing to pass the tests becomes a real ordeal. It is a two-day exam, both written and oral, and could cover our knowledge of the Polish language and European literature, as well as the Latin and German languages. It will include mathematics and may also include many of the sciences: biology, chemistry, and physics; plus geography, ancient history, and philosophy. Rumor has it that they may also question us about art history or music history.

Even if we do pass, we know that for Jews it is now becoming virtually impossible to study medicine at the university. If we work very hard we can study engineering, law, languages, or education. We do not have the same rights as gentiles and we know there is nothing we can do about it but try to succeed against the odds.

In 1934, thirty students in my graduating class take the Matura. On Monday we have a four-hour written exam. Then Tuesday is the oral exam. As I walk, exhausted, out of the examination room, I see my father standing in the hall, waiting to hear the results.

I can't believe my eyes. Until this moment I have had no idea how much Tatte really cares about me. I have never felt especially noticed or appreciated by him. I am his child and I know he loves me like he loves all his children but I am nothing special or unique. Now I feel a sudden shock and then a warm glow when I see my papa at the school, and on a business day! Finally, I understand how much he really loves me and that he is very proud of me.

Only seven of the thirty students pass, and I am one of those seven. This is such an important accomplishment that years later I hear it had been reported in a newspaper in Jerusalem!

Fortunately, none of my twenty-three classmates who fail the exam commit suicide. The year before, several students had killed themselves because they hadn't passed the Matura.

Love

My beloved is clear-skinned and ruddy,
Preeminent among ten thousand.
His head is finest gold,
His locks are curled
And black as a raven . . .
His mouth is delicious
And all of him is delightful,
Such is my beloved,
Such is my darling,
O maidens of Jerusalem!
—Song of Solomon 5:10–11, 16

1931–1933

From a very young age I have been close friends with Sala Grinzspan and Rozia Nissenson. Rozia is a striking girl, with dark brown eyes and bouncing black curls. I think Sala is quite beautiful. She has thick, curly blond hair and blue eyes. It is because of Sala that I first become aware of Heniek Wajshof.

The first day I entered the Gymnasium in the sixth grade I noticed Heniek. Although he is short, Heniek stands out because he is extremely smart, suave, and funny. He has sparkly bright blue eyes and wavy brown hair and is popular with all the girls, as well as the boys. Even at just twelve, he had a reputation for dating younger girls and then quickly dropping them. And I was immediately warned to be careful of my heart with him.

I don't really pay too much attention to Heniek until I am fifteen. That fall, Sala develops a crush on Srulek, Heniek's cousin, and she makes me stay near her at school as she tries to get Srulek's attention. Because Heniek and his cousin are always together, I see Heniek every day and I start to like him. He is so witty. He always makes me laugh, but I know that he never notices me.

On the day of the first snowfall in early November 1931, I am walking home with Sala and we see Rozia with Heniek. We start throwing snowballs at her, and Heniek throws a snowball directly at me. It hits me very hard in my face and I know that he hates me. I run home and cry bitter tears of disappointment quietly into my pillow.

Months later, there is a spring dance at school. Heniek asks Rozia if I am going to go. Rozia knows that I feel too shy to go and, to protect me, tells Heniek that I can't go because I don't have the right thing to wear.

"Well, Gucia could wear her blue sweater," he says. "She looks lovely in that."

When Rozia tells me his words, I am shocked. Not only has he noticed me, but he thinks I am pretty! I am thrilled and immediately imagine myself going to the dance. I would enter the auditorium feeling confident in my blue sweater, my spirits lifted even higher by the music and dancing. Heniek would see me and come over to invite me to dance.

And then I freeze. Because I realize that he would know Rozia had told me about their conversation and there I would be, wearing my blue sweater for him. I am much too proud to make such a blatant declaration of my feelings. Worse yet, what if he understands all of that and doesn't even ask me to dance? I would be standing there watching him dance with other girls, feeling like a fool. I feel myself blush at the mere thought of it. Maybe if I had planned on going all along it could have turned out to be the most magical evening of my life. I feel sick at the spot I have boxed myself into, but under the circumstances, going to the dance is impossible.

I spend the evening of the dance at home, in a state of turmoil. All night I ricochet between misery and longing over what I am missing, and joy at the secret knowledge that Heniek likes me.

After that, nothing changes on the outside, but everything feels different when we see each other at school. Now I see that his jokes and comments, as several of us stand together talking, are directed at me. I would never say that I become bold with him, but I certainly relax around him and am able to enjoy the attention that I've never before even let myself notice.

Our common dedication to Zionism gives us more opportunities to be in each other's company. These days, everyone belongs to a youth group, but there are striking ideological differences among us. Like every Zionist youth group, Hanoar Hatzioni believes that the only way to keep Jewish culture alive in the world is to create a Jewish state in Palestine. But it rejects all political ideologies as divisive. Sala, Rozia, and I feel we have outgrown it and want just the opposite. We want a higher purpose to believe in, a cause that would benefit not just Jews but all of mankind.

Along with Heniek and Srulek and many of our friends, we join Hashomer Hatsair (the Youth Guard), a left-wing Zionist organization named after a group formed in Palestine in 1909. Itka is in a religious group called Bet Yaakov. There is another group, called Betar, the youth organization of the right-wing Jabotinsky Revisionists, but we think their ideas are too radical. Our group is committed to creating a Jewish state in Palestine peacefully, buying up land bit by bit, and establishing a socialist society. But the Revisionists mock us for thinking you can buy a country. They believe the way to reclaim Eretz Yisrael—the Holy Land—is to fight for it. Then you can worry about how to run it.

Hashomer Hatsair is much more fun than Hanoar Hatzioni was. At least twice a week we meet at the Maccabee Sports Club, a large building with many halls for the meetings of different Zionist groups. There is a huge backyard where we learn to dance and sing Israeli songs.

Soon after joining, I am chosen as leader of my own *kvuca*, a group of seven girls, all about four years younger than I. In our meetings, we are given discussion assignments: the history of Zionism, the history and traditions of Eretz Yisrael. Often our leaders will call a meeting of all the groups, boys and girls together.

At some point I am chosen to deliver a speech to the entire group on the origins of Zionism. I am terrified as I picture myself speaking with so many eyes on me. And, to make it worse, Heniek will be there.

How I research and study for that speech, spending long hours in the library poring over old dusty books written in Hebrew, chewing the erasers off my pencils, and my fingernails as well!

On the day of my speech I can't eat a thing. I am shaking inside and out. I pray that I won't make a fool of myself; that people will think my ideas are intelligent and interesting; that my voice won't quake. I decide to wear my favorite outfit, a blue silk skirt and the same blue sweater Heniek had admired me wearing. But still I am so self-conscious about how I look. It is winter, and although I have put Nivea cream on my nose every day, it is still as red as borscht. I know it is a sin, but I put Coty powder on my nose to hide the redness. I try to do it discreetly. It is okay for Hela to use powder because she is older, but it is not okay for me. Anyway, she has left her powder on her table near our bed and I use it.

As I walk to the podium, I am grateful that my long blue skirt hides my knees because they are knocking together as I start to speak. But once I begin I settle down. I get caught up in the ideas and beliefs that mean so much to me and I actually enjoy myself.

When the meeting is over, a lot of the members gather around me and are very enthusiastic in congratulating me. I am a bit embarrassed by all the compliments but privately quite pleased. And then Heniek tells me that my speech was perfect! I don't have any idea what I say to him, but I do know how dry my mouth feels, how sweaty my hands are, and how happy I am.

After that Heniek is more direct in seeking me out. We spend more and more time together. While before we were together mostly as part of a small group of friends, over the next two weeks we start being with each other, just the two of us, talking after meetings, walking home from school, and taking evening strolls around the main square. I can hardly concentrate on my schoolwork. All I think about is when we will be together again. And then one evening, as he walks me home, he declares his feelings for me. I tell him I feel the same way, and we are officially in love.

(They call us the Golden Couple, and little do I know that these will be the happiest years of my life.)

Even though I study such long hours and so hard that my vision blurs and my head spins, my life is charged with meaning and purpose and dreams. I am in love and smart and a leader and admired by my peers.

After rushing to finish my homework, twice a week I go to Hashomer Hatsair meetings where Heniek and I can see each other, and the rest of the time we go out walking. On those nights I turn off the light in my bedroom as a sign that my homework is finished. Heniek is waiting on the street for me, watching my window. When the light goes off he knows that I will soon be downstairs. We walk a few blocks to go strolling in the Bernardynski Garden and Plac Czarnieckiego. A lot of people are there, Poles and Jews alike. We call it our *shpetzia*, our promenade. It is so romantic to go walking with Heniek, arm in arm, joking and laughing, meeting our friends and looking at the old people gossiping on the park benches.

The passionate commitment to Zionism that Heniek and I share adds fuel to our romance. Often on our walks we carry little blue cans with a small slot on top and ask people to donate a few coins for the pioneers struggling to eke out a living as they devote themselves to building Eretz Yisrael. The can is called a *puszka*. Most Jews have one. As long as I can remember, Mama has kept a can for the Jewish orphanage on the kitchen windowsill. Giving money to others less fortunate is one of the 613 *mitzvot* Jews must perform, and we are glad to be working for a cause we care about so deeply. We are bursting with vitality, imagining a future bright with possibilities. Whatever our choices, they will be in the service of our dream to build a Jewish homeland in Palestine.

When it grows colder, Heniek comes to visit at my house. Sometimes we sit in the parlor and I help him with his class in mathematical discussion. He is so bright and good in school and has planned to be a lawyer from the time he was a little boy. But his mind is just not as quick in math as mine. Because I've always looked up to him for how smart and knowledgeable he is, I am grateful for this chance to earn his respect.

Hela often has her friends over at the same time, meeting in our dining room. Sometimes it is just her boyfriend, Jacob Brem, but often it is his weekly card game with his best friend, Leon Reichmann, and some of the others from their right-wing Zionist youth group, Betar. Of course Heniek and I have nothing to do with them. Besides being about five years older than we are, they have political views that are the opposite of ours and we have nothing in common. They really seem to know how to have fun, though. I don't understand how they can be so playful and lighthearted, cracking jokes and teasing each other, and at the same time believe in a branch of Zionism that promotes violence as the means to create a Jewish state.

Hela has our maid, Janova, bring them dish after dish of food that Hela has set aside from our family meals. I think this is terribly selfish and wrong. And besides that, I am embarrassed in front of Heniek.

Heniek's father works for the Community Council; he is not paid very well and the Wajshofs don't have a lot of money. I don't want Heniek to see such extravagance. I am afraid that he might feel uncomfortable seeing how well off we are, and I get really angry at Hela for putting me in this awkward position. Except for buying us tickets to the latest Hollywood picture at Flattau's Movie Theater, Heniek doesn't need money for our dates, nor do we have time for much else beyond the demands of school and Hashomer Hatsair. Plus, I don't want to cater to Heniek like Hela serves Jacob. Our relationship is built on total equality.

One of the highlights of our Zionist meetings is when a man named David Ben-Gurion comes to speak to all the different organizations. He was born in Poland but lives in Palestine, where he heads the trade union he founded to organize Jewish workers in Palestine. We are told that in 1909 he organized Hashomer (the Guild of Watchmen) as a self-defense organization for the Jews in Palestine and we are thrilled to meet him, especially because our group was named after his group.

Members of some of the other groups, like Betar and Bet Yaakov, are not as excited or honored by Ben-Gurion's visit.

This short, sturdy, middle-aged man with thick dark eyebrows and lots of bushy white hair in an electrified circle around his head eloquently talks about the socialism and equality and happiness in Israel. He tells us we must all work very hard to buy back the land and we must go there to be farmers like our ancestors, to be pioneers for Zion.

Suddenly the mood changes. An older leader of the far-right Jabotinsky Revisionists starts heckling Ben-Gurion, shouting loudly that Ben-Gurion and his ilk are cowards and Communists and that we Jews must take the land back by force, as it was taken from our ancestors fifteen hundred years ago. Then the Jabotinsky leader's cohorts, including the younger members of Betar, join in, jeering and yelling at Ben-Gurion. I see Jews from my town whom I vaguely know, right-wingers like Leon Reichmann and his cousin Henry Marton, Sabina Markowitz, Sala Jacobowitz, and others, jumping up and rudely screaming. Soon some of our members from Hashomer Hatsair join in and start shouting back. And then suddenly the older Jabotinsky leader strikes one of the men, yelling at him. That man hits back, and in no time at all fists are flying. Even Heniek and Srulek jump into this enormous brawl. It shocks and saddens me that we Zionists, we Jews, would fight each other with such anger and hatred. (I would never imagine that in the future destiny will intertwine our lives with such love.)

I know there is a passionate rivalry among the different Zionist factions, but I have little interest in any of that. For me Zionism means camaraderie, devotion to a shared cause, and enthusiastic, high-spirited fun. During the summers that I am fifteen, sixteen, and seventeen, our Hashomer Hatsair group goes away to camp for two weeks. We ride in carriages pulled by horses and stay in little houses in the country.

Heniek and the other boys are in one house, Sala, Rozia, and I, and the rest of the girls in another. We are all given jobs to do.

My first job is to make the morning coffee for everyone. I have never had to cook in my life. All I know about coffee is that it needs to be dark. Because of the Depression, people try to economize wherever they can, and real coffee is stretched by mixing it with the ground roots of a more readily available plant called chicory. But I don't know that. So I grind up a lot of beans—a lot—which makes the coffee not only very dark but also so bitter and vile that no one can drink it and we have to throw it away. I am mortified and think that Heniek will never want to marry me because I am such a bad cook.

At summer camp we talk a lot about Zionism and Israel and sing Hebrew songs and dance Israeli dances. We also play little games. One day we girls are sitting in a circle, and the game is to write anonymous notes to each other. I receive a note that says, *Don't bother with Heniek. He will drop you. He will break your heart.*

This "warning" infuriates me. People hear rumors and take as fact what they wish to believe. But I know that Heniek loves me and will stay with me, and that the girl who wrote the note is probably just jealous. I never play that game again.

At camp and at our twice-weekly meetings during the school year, we have doctors and lawyers and professors come to our groups and talk with great fervor about Zionism. To live in Israel is to achieve the pinnacle of happiness and to fulfill our Jewish destiny. The speeches are enthralling, painting a picture of the glorious lives we will create in Israel. It will be a socialist country where everyone will be equal and we will all take care of one another in peace and freedom. Israel will be a country where we Jews will no longer be persecuted. When anti-Semites scream, "Go back to your own country," we will actually have a country to go back to. We will live our lives together with one communal purpose. We will at last return to the land of Abraham and Isaac and Jacob. Though we Jews had been farmers and shepherds for centuries, now many parts of Europe have laws preventing us from owning land. As a result most of us live in the big cities and villages and have forgotten our roots; we have forgotten how to love the land.

One of the lecturers keeps talking about Israel as so perfect, so pure, such an ideal climate that I am unable to stop myself. "Poland has great beauty, too," I blurt out.

He is furious with me. I wonder why he has to make Israel such a utopia. What faults is he hiding from us? Are our leaders whitewashing any flaws from the image they are creating for us, even at the cost of the truth?

Some of my friends go to Israel to study. They are so excited, thinking it will be all they want or need in life, but many come back disappointed. They report that life there is primitive and hard. I start to question much of what we've been told and encouraged to believe. I even wonder if Hashomer Hatsair is intentionally trying to indoctrinate us with propaganda, fearing that an honest portrayal of life in Palestine would discourage us from going there as pioneers.

It becomes clear that life on a *kibbutz*, an agricultural commune where everyone lives and works together in true equality, means abandoning our personal ambitions and desires and obeying the values and dreams and orders and rules set by others. Of course, since the time I was four and walked out of kindergarten, I've known I wasn't very good at passively submitting to any situation that made no sense to me.

Slowly, painfully, I come to understand that I can never go to Israel to live on a *kibbutz* where I would have to subjugate myself to an outside authority with the power to dictate my work, my hours. I need the freedom to choose my own course in life.

I fear Herzl's words that I "shall live at last as free," which I had memorized, are not the personal reality that awaits me.

Heniek and I spend many hours privately grappling with our doubts while publicly continuing in our leadership positions. Finally, when I am eighteen, after much soul-searching, and even though I am the secretary of the group, I leave the organization that I have loved as a part of my very being and that has provided such meaning and pleasure and direction throughout my teenage years.

The Rabbi

Once there was a gentile who came before the sage Hillel and said to him: "Convert me to Judaism on the condition that you teach me the whole Torah while I stand on one foot." Hillel converted him, saying: "What is hateful to you, do not do to your fellow man. This is the whole Torah; the rest is the explanation. Go and learn."
—Hillel the Elder (110 BCE–10 CE)

1934–1935

Poland is recovering from the Great Depression, but painfully slowly. Like all the others, my family is having a hard time financially. Mama and Papa decide to open another butcher store, this time for gentiles. My parents realize that they don't need to sell the back half of their perfectly good meat to the gentile butchers at wholesale just because those cuts aren't kosher. Why not just open a second store and sell those non-kosher parts directly to the gentile customers? After all, they are also some of the more choice cuts of meat. This turns out to be a good idea, and the new butcher store is quickly successful.

Soon after that Mama decides we can earn more profit from our kosher stock by making and selling delicatessen meats. There is only one kosher delicatessen in Piotrków. It is owned by Pan Korman, and it is on the other side of town. A small store space has just become available on the ground floor of our building. Mama hires a gentile man and teaches him how to make kosher salamis from the end pieces of the kosher meat. How I love the delicious smells and tastes of those deli meats. I bring them to school with me and look forward to our snack break all morning.

But Pan Korman, obviously, does not want the competition. He is a very influential Hasid who gives a lot of money to the religious community, so he and his business friends go to the rabbis to protest. Even though Mama strictly follows all the laws of *kashruth* in preparing the meats, the rabbis refuse to certify them kosher. We have no choice but to close the shop. Mama and Tatte are so disappointed to lose the new business. I am disappointed to lose all that delicious food. We are all angry at the unfairness of the decision.

We also can no longer afford two live-in maids. Since Krysia's parents are old and sick, she decides to go back to her village. It seems very strange not to have her in my life anymore. I have known her since I was born.

Early in 1934 we hear that Piotrków will be getting a new chief rabbi. Mama decides we can economize by renting our own large, beautiful apartment to the rabbi's family and moving into the Nissensons' smaller apartment across the hall.

In September, just before the High Holidays, we move into Rozia's apartment. I feel guilty that we are making the Nissensons move out and that my best friend won't be across the hall anymore. Also, I am sorry to lose our balconies, where I love to sunbathe and watch the lively street scene below. I have to content myself with the view of the backyard and the gazebo and my dear old apple tree. Fortunately, the outhouse is not part of the view.

Soon after we move out of our apartment, my sister Hela and Jacob get married and move to the little apartment down the hall from us on the other side of the staircase. I am happy for Hela because she is so much in love with Jacob, and it looks like they will have a very nice life together. Jacob's father has an extremely successful business—a small factory in town that produces ready-made clothes for the Polish people living in the villages. (The people in town who can afford better don't buy ready-made clothes. Like us, they all go to tailors.) Jacob works with his father. He is in charge of sending salesmen to the countryside to sell the clothes to the peasants.

I am happy that Hela and Jacob are living in the little apartment for another reason. Now I will have my own bed and room. But I am the happiest of all because the crazy man who was living in Hela's new apartment is forced to move out. Pan Herszkowicz had lived in that apartment since I was a little child and he used to terrorize me with his howling. At any time of the day or night he might start screaming out that he was "the King." Sometimes, when I would come home from school, the whole hallway would be completely pasted over with black paper. My parents told me he was harmless, but if that was true, why did Pan Herszkowicz's mother and wife leave cooked food in front of his door, knock loudly, and then quickly run away? They would never go into his apartment or even wait for him to open the door.

All of us are looking forward to going to the Great Synagogue for the evening of Yom Kippur, because we will finally get to see the new rabbi, Moshe Chaim Lau. We've been waiting for months. Everyone has already heard that he is a very learned scholar and a charming, dynamic speaker. Both he and his wife come from long lines of eminent, legendary rabbis going back centuries; on her side even including Rashi, one of Judaism's most important scholars and authorities. The Laus are eager to return to Poland and establish their permanent family home in Piotrków.

We have heard, too, of his extraordinary bravery and strength of will. Nine months ago, while still chief rabbi of Prešov, Czechoslovakia, he had begun a fund-raising mission for the Hachmei Lublin Yeshiva, and it was during his stop in Piotrków that he was offered and accepted the post of chief rabbi. This was big news, as the post had been vacant for two years. But because of a terrible accident, we had to wait many more months for our new rabbi: just as Rabbi Lau was re-boarding the train at his next stop in Kraków, it lurched forward. The rabbi went flying out the open door. He landed on his back between the rails of the track, beneath the moving train. To protect his head, he covered it with his right arm, and as the wheels rolled over him, they mangled his right elbow. He was rushed to the hospital, but the doctors weren't able to save his arm. They had to amputate it just above the crushed elbow.

Now, standing before us in his white High Holiday robes, which hide his missing arm, we see a tall, good-looking, healthy man with a neatly trimmed light brown beard and mustache and rimless glasses. Sitting behind the rabbi, on little stools facing the congregation, are his two darling sons: ten-year-old Naphtali (Tulek) and seven-year-old Shmuel Yitzhak (Milek). Rabbi Lau gives such a beautiful and moving service that I have goose bumps on my arms and tears in my eyes.

After the holidays are over, the Laus move into our old apartment. We learn that both the rabbi and his wife, Rebbitzin Chaya Lau, are originally from Kraków. She is sophisticated and elegant and, like my mama, intelligent and warm, extremely beautiful, and always well dressed.

Two years later, Hela and Jacob have a son, Marek, and Chaya Lau has her third son, Yisrael (Lulek). By that time the rebbitzin and I have become good friends. There is always a commotion in her home, people coming to consult with the rabbi on religious matters or to settle disputes. So to escape the chaos, Rebbitzin Lau comes to us across the hall to visit, bringing the new baby and maid with her. Even though Mama is at the store, the rebbitzin seems to enjoy sitting around the table with my friends and me, content that Hela and the maid are taking good care of the babies. We discuss all sorts of things, politics and philosophy and even a little local gossip. For me she is like a window into the larger world, even into the future. And best of all, she is happy to let me use her balcony to sunbathe.

(Little do I know that it will be Rebbitzin Lau whose advice and love will later help me save my life.)

The University

A University should be a place of light, of liberty,
and of learning.
—Benjamin Disraeli (1804–1881)

1937

On the one hand, passing the Matura makes me think the world is mine. I am so exhilarated and actually feel taller, as if a heavy weight has been lifted from my shoulders. It is the culmination of all my efforts toward achieving my goals.

On the other hand, I am so mentally and physically exhausted after the rigorous ordeal of going to school six days a week and then the intense stress of studying and worrying about the Matura, that I spend the next three years doing very little. Perhaps I am lazy, but I really can't do much of anything at this time, and luckily, I don't have to. Tatte and Mama say their businesses are good enough that I don't need to work. Janova helps Mama with all the housecleaning and the cooking. I spend most evenings with Heniek, who is busy during the day working as an apprentice for a lawyer here in Piotrków. He wants to practice law but studying at the university is very expensive, and he hopes to learn enough this way to pass the qualifying exam. I haven't had so much free time and so few responsibilities since I was a small child.

I do a little tutoring, though this has gotten off to a bad start. My first student is a young Jewish girl. It is frustrating work because she is very slow and spoiled. I wonder if this has to do with the circumstances of her birth. Her mother is the sister of the father's first wife, who died in childbirth. A year after this second marriage, they had this little girl. I think maybe in their grief her parents overindulged her, and although it is hard to tutor her, I feel sorry for them and am happy to help. I tutor her for a month, but when I ask for my wages, the father refuses to pay me. I am furious but say nothing and leave. I should have expected it. People in town had said he was untrustworthy. Sometime later I learn that this dishonest man has gone bankrupt and has had to leave town in shame.

"Well, see, there is justice in this world, after all," I say to Heniek, when we hear that news.

And this is also when the Dobranski family asks me to tutor their son. They live in a very small, simple cottage just next to the fence at the back of our property. As poor as they are, I am paid for every single lesson. And I get a cup of good hot tea as well.

So I spend these three wonderful last years of my innocence just taking life easy, reading, going to the movies, and walking with Heniek.

Sometimes I get bored with him and tell him we need time apart. We stop seeing each other and then we both suffer terribly. He writes the most wonderfully romantic and witty letters to me and then we get back together again. I care for him deeply but . . . this dream of real love . . . this love that we see in the movies . . . this love we read of in books, I am never sure if what I feel for Heniek is true love. At first when he held my hand I would get goose bumps all over. But now, after five years together, I feel almost nothing at all.

My mama who married for love, my mama who refused to go to a matchmaker and chose my father on her own, who never criticizes any of us or tells us what to do (though we always know where she stands), has made only one comment about my relationship. She says that if Heniek and I marry, what with me being five feet two inches and him only five feet five, we will have short children. But I ignore her concern. Heniek's height doesn't bother me at all, nor does the fact that at eighteen he was already losing his curly brown hair. With his great sense of humor, his suave personality, his wit, charisma, and intelligence, I just look into his bright blue eyes and melt. We are so comfortable together. We never fight or argue. But I do get bored. Maybe that is the problem: the fire has gone out.

When the fall weather makes it uncomfortable for us to walk in the park, we go to the library to read or to Heniek's house to listen to the radio. It was at Heniek's, back in 1933, that I first heard the voice and words of Adolf Hitler.

It was January 30, and the president of Germany, Von Hindenburg, had appointed an Austrian Nazi named Adolf Hitler to be the chancellor of Germany. Immediately Hitler started making hateful speeches against the Jews. We could feel his charisma over the radio and Heniek and I knew from the cheering, enthusiastic crowds how hypnotized the Germans were.

On that day, religious Jews all over Poland, like Itka Ber's father, proclaimed a day of praying and fasting. (A lot of good that did. There are many days to come when we will go without food, and not as an act of religious piety.)

That April we learned that Hitler was calling for the Germans to boycott all Jewish shops and businesses. A lot of gentiles who had usually shopped at Jewish stores in Germany began to stay away. I had always loved the German language, but little by little, hearing Hitler's voice on the radio, I started to hate and fear it. More and more, the radio told us of new, hateful, anti-Semitic laws in Germany. Jews could no longer work in government jobs like the post office or state or city agencies or teach at the universities. Then, on a beautiful spring day in May of 1933, we were horrified to hear that thousands of books written by Jews and Communists had been piled in the streets of Berlin and burned, with crowds cheering and fanning the flames and throwing in more and more books.

Hitler kept screaming that the Germans needed *Lebensraum*—living space. He said that the superior Aryan race was entitled to more land. Hitler said they would soon take back the German-speaking Sudetenland in Czechoslovakia, and after that, Germany would take back Austria as well. As the German national anthem proclaimed, it was "Deutschland über alles"—Germany, above all.

"And what about Poland?" we asked one another, horrified at the possibility.

That hot July we learned that Jews who had immigrated to Germany from Poland and other Eastern European countries had lost their German citizenship; Hitler said that Jews from Eastern Europe could never again be considered German.

In our hearts, in our souls, I guess we all knew from the beginning that there would be a war. We knew that Hitler would come to Poland. But we just couldn't believe it. Heniek and I decided we must put our fears aside and look forward: we would talk about our dreams for the future. We believed the future was still ours to control.

I know I want to get a university education, but I can't make up my mind. I still want to go to Palestine but certainly not to live on a *kibbutz*. So I apply to the famous Hebrew University on Mount Scopus in Jerusalem, and I am accepted! My mama cries when I receive my acceptance letter.

She is very proud of me and buys me a lovely ring with a sparkling ruby, but I know she can't stand the idea that I will be so far away from her. And I am concerned about how expensive it will be. We have recovered from the Depression and my parents can now afford it; still, I feel guilty asking them to pay the high tuition. My parents never say no to any of their children, but I know it would be selfish of me to go to Mount Scopus.

I am happy for Sala that she was able to move to Israel to study, but not because of why she had to leave. She is still in love with Heniek's cousin Srulek, but she suffered terribly for that love. Srulek took Sala for granted and flirted openly with other women. She forced herself to end the relationship but sank into a deep depression in her grief. Her family thought distance would help mend her broken heart, so with their encouragement, she moved to Eretz Yisrael and enrolled in the Technion in Haifa.

Since Sala left Piotrków, Srulek has continued to visit with Heniek and other friends and they often gather at my house. But I miss Sala and it is strange to be with Srulek without her; he is in such high spirits, as though nothing is different. (At the time I am unable to guess that what then seemed to Sala like such a tragedy is the great luck that saves her life!)

Eventually I start to grow restless and am ready to get on with my future. To our great disappointment, Heniek fails the examination to qualify as a lawyer. He enrolls to study law at the Józef Piłsudskiego University in Warsaw, so it seems natural to go on with my education and join him there, as well. Around this time, Srulek comes to my apartment on his own and he suggests that I apply to the Jagiellonian University in Kraków. He is studying chemistry there and thinks it would be a great experience for me to live in such a lovely city as Kraków. He says that English is going to be very popular and important and I should study it.

I want to test my independence and I think it would be a good idea to try a separation from Heniek. Being apart, I can see if what I feel for Heniek is true love or not. Of course Heniek is not happy about this, he says how much he'll miss me; but he agrees that if we are meant to be together for the rest of our lives, our bond should be strong enough to endure a year apart.

So, at the age of twenty-one, I decide to apply to the university in Kraków and live away from Heniek and the only home I've ever had.

Mama thinks it is a wonderful idea and urges me to go. Now that Jacob has been drafted into the Polish army, Hela will be all alone with her new baby, Marek, and Regina is only eleven, so Mama says she will have enough children to get hugs from. And Kraków is not far away like Israel. I can come home whenever I want.

Kraków is part of Galician Poland, a city of more cultured, educated, higher-class Poles. It has a more Austrian-like standard of living and all our teachers at the Gymnasium were from there. I am delighted when I am accepted.

Fortunately, I find lodging through an ad in the newspaper placed by Itka Moskowitz, a girl I had known slightly from Piotrków. She is already a sophomore at Jagiellonian University and is happy to have a friend from Piotrków to share the room she is renting in a private home in the Jewish quarter. In Kraków, the Jewish boys have a dormitory, as do the gentile girls and boys, but there is no place for the Jewish girls. The Jewish family we live with does not allow us to use the kitchen (I suppose they don't trust us to be perfectly kosher) so we have to eat out all the time. My family often sends me food packages from home: delicious coffee cakes and pies and cookies and Hela always makes my favorite, her special paté.

In the classes, we Jews know that we have to sit in the back of the classroom and keep to ourselves, but I love going to the university.

The classes are so stimulating and I am thrilled to learn English. I love the sound of it and the freedom of the grammar and the wide choice of vocabulary. I have never studied that language before, so it is extremely hard and I am never without my dictionary. But I think, soon I will be able to read Shakespeare, and that keeps me going. My favorite teacher is Professor Dybowski. He is ordinary looking but his intellect and enthusiastic love of English make him attractive.

The years of worry and hard work preparing for the Matura have taught me how to think and write and learn. Now I am able to enjoy my classes without all that pressure and without all those boring hours of Hebrew studies and memorization. I have much more time for myself, and living on my own away from home for the first time, I feel free. So even though my studies are challenging, I find my first year at the university easier than the Gymnasium.

It is exciting to meet other Jewish students from different parts of Poland and to sit for hours drinking glasses of tea and debating ideas and strolling around the main square where musicians play Chopin—the great Polish composer—for the coins people toss into their cups. Soon after I arrive in Kraków, Srulek asks me to go to the movies and I invite Itka to join us. The next time he asks me, he says I shouldn't bring Itka, so I understand that he is interested in me not just as a friend. I am disgusted. I tell him I don't feel comfortable leaving Itka out, that it would be rude. He doesn't ask again. Does he think I would consider him, after he has broken my best friend's heart? And how could he pursue his own cousin's girlfriend? I think of what Sala or Heniek would feel if they knew of such a betrayal, and I think that Sala's heartbreak is nothing to what she would have suffered if she'd stayed with him.

*　*　*

75

That year in Kraków without Heniek makes me realize how much I miss him. I decide to transfer to the university in Warsaw for my second year, and Heniek is thrilled. He encourages me and says he can get me some work tutoring to help with the tuition. I apply to the university and am accepted. That September, Heniek and I take the train together from Piotrków to Warsaw, where I become a second-year student at the university. Heniek finds me a room to rent in the home of a religious family on Twarda Street, just next to a synagogue. The family is quite nice to me and they trust me to use their kitchen, but whenever the old grandfather hears me go into the kitchen (his room is next to it) he quickly comes in. He wears an old, torn *yarmulke* and has an unkempt, greasy beard, and he leers at me. As I am making my tea or coffee, he pinches my bottom. I just hate that so much that I stop going into the kitchen and once again have to eat all my meals out.

I am not as happy as I had been rooming with Itka Moskowitz in Kraków, but at least Heniek and I can see each other, and the classes are marvelous. I study English, of course, as well as the history of philosophy, and Old English. We read *Beowulf* and Chaucer. The Old English is so much like German that those classes are the easiest.

Compared to my English professor in Kraków, whom I looked up to with such high regard, Professor Tretiak in Warsaw is a very different sort. One day, I start to enter his office during student hours, but stop short. Sitting on his lap is a girl from my class who always sits in the front row and wears lots of heavy makeup. Luckily, they don't see me, and I leave very quietly. After getting over my shock, I realize that here at the university there is much to learn outside the classroom as well as inside it. I had always credited people who were intelligent and educated with high morals. But now I understand that character and intellect are not the same thing.

Because of the increasing difficulty for Jews to pass the Matura, there are not a lot of us attending the university, and there is even more anti-Semitism in Warsaw than in Kraków. The Polish political party called Endecja is represented on the campus. We have seen them in Piotrków, carrying signs that say: MOSZKU IDZ DO PALESTYNY! (KIKES TO PALESTINE!). In fact, Endecja had proposed that the Piotrków City Council make a symbolic gesture of allocating one *zloty* from the city budget to help in a voluntary mass immigration of the Jews of Piotrków to Palestine. They wanted to show how much they hate Jews and want us all to leave.

In support of the Jews, who are one-third of the population of Piotrków, the council refused Endecja that symbolic *zloty*. And, since Endecja is made up of such a small group of Poles, we all ignored them.

But that was in Piotrków. Now, in Warsaw, I start to feel directly threatened. At the university, the members of Endecja carry out campaigns called "Days Without Jews," meaning no Jews are allowed on the campus for days, weeks, or months. Often they stand at the gates to the university and make us show our identification cards, which have ZHID stamped on them. The members of Endecja scrutinize the card of anyone they think looks Jewish. Then they beat up those Jews who try to enter to go to classes. Jewish blood runs over the cobblestones of the courtyard.

The most frightening part is that there is no one to protect us. The police are not allowed to interfere on the campus, where they have no jurisdiction. I am filled with a sense of helplessness and outrage that the university permits this injustice.

Somehow the people in Endecja do not guess that Heniek and I are Jews. They never demand to see our identification cards and they always let us through, but each time I have to pass by them, I tremble, my stomach churning with fear. I am particularly worried about Heniek because they are brutal to the men, but he just smiles and tells jokes and they never stop him.

Once, in my history of philosophy class, we have an oral test. The teacher calls the students into a room in pairs. The boy I am with answers all the questions exactly as I do, but he has brown eyes, dark curly hair, a large nose, and a Jewish name. The professor points to me and says to the boy, "Pani Gomolinska said it right and you didn't. You have failed."

I feel so terrible for him. It is his third try at that test and because he fails, he has to leave the university.

With my light hair, rosy cheeks, and Polish name, I pass.

Passover

Passover has a message for the conscience and the heart of all mankind.
For what does it commemorate? It commemorates the deliverance
of a people from degrading slavery, from most foul and cruel tyranny.
And so, it is Israel's—nay, God's protest against unrighteousness,
whether individual or national.
—Rabbi Morris Joseph (1848–1930)

APRIL 1939

We all know our history—that Jews have long been considered different and have often been hated and feared. We are used to living with discrimination and inferior rights. On occasion the ever-present virus of anti-Semitism erupts into violent persecution and we are subjected to pogroms and exile. In my personal experience, it is simply an unfortunate fact of life, which we Jews have learned to accept and endure, like putting up with a bad cold or too many days of snow.

I have always loved Passover because it is such a beautiful affirmation of the triumph of the Jews over our oppressors. We rejoice in the victory of our ancestors who went out of Egypt where they had been horribly degraded by slavery and indignities. We recite from the

Haggadah, the book retelling the story of the anguish of our bondage: that by many miracles of God, Moses was sent to free us from slavery and lead us to the Promised Land.

But because of the increasingly horrifying news coming out of Germany, Passover of 1939 is terribly different from any other I have experienced.

After Hitler became chancellor in 1933 and then führer in 1934, he had decreed that the army must swear its full allegiance to him and only him.

In September 1934, the Nuremberg Laws—anti-Jewish laws—were enacted. No Jews, even if they had lived in Germany for four generations, were allowed to fly the German flag in front of their houses. Jews had already been excluded from the army and so many professions. It was difficult for Jews to go to medical school in Poland, but not impossible. In Germany, in 1936, Jewish doctors were forbidden from practicing medicine in German hospitals.

By the end of 1936, Heniek and I had started hearing rumors that anti-Hitler Germans and Communists, Gypsies, Jehovah's Witnesses, homosexuals, disabled people, and Jews were being rounded up and sent away to "concentration camps."

Suddenly my eyes are wide open and I see new images of persecution. I listen to the Seder story with new ears and taste all the foods with a new tongue. It makes me feel depressed and afraid.

But I don't think of these things when I first wake up on the morning of the Seder. I start out in a happy mood. I am home from the university in Warsaw for a week and able to rest my brain. It's so much fun being in the kitchen with Mama and Janova, and I am actually going to help prepare the food. Of course, because of my reputation as a terrible cook, I am given only two jobs, and watched very closely at that.

I will decorate the Seder tray and finish making the *charoset*. As I carefully place the ritual foods on the Seder plate, for the first time the Passover story strikes me as not just symbolic but frighteningly real.

The large white china tray has six circular spaces. In one I put the *maror*—the bitter herbs—the horseradish, which will remind us of the bitter lives of our ancestors when they were slaves in Egypt. In the next circle, I put the *karpas*—some spring onions, radishes, and parsley, because Passover is a celebration of spring and rebirth. It is a joyous holiday promising us new, fresh, and happy beginnings. I carefully place the bowl of salt water in the center of the tray so that we can dip our herbs in that water to remind us of the tears the Jewish slaves shed in their misery and bondage in Egypt.

The *charoset* is from a recipe of my mother's mother, who died when I was very little. Janova has just peeled and cored the apples and it is my job to help her by chopping them up with almonds and raisins and a little cinnamon and some wine. I try to keep the *charoset* dry because it symbolizes the mortar the Jews used when, as slaves, they were laying bricks for the pharaoh.

It is almost sundown. The *matzo* balls are bouncing in the chicken soup and the smells from the kitchen are the smells of heaven. To complete the tray I place a burned bone from the lower part of the front leg of a lamb, representing the Paschal Lamb. This bone symbolizes the spring lamb God ordered our ancestors to sacrifice to Him and eat before they fled Egypt. And last, a hard-boiled egg that has been scorched—another ancient spring symbol of the renewal of life. Carefully I take the Seder tray to the table. We will begin our celebration in half an hour.

There is a knock on the door and my mother's favorite brother, Josef Libeskind, his wife, Sura, their son, Janek, and their young daughters, Mala and Rozia, come to wish us a happy Pesach. They are on their way to celebrate Passover at the house of their oldest daughter, Mania. The family has gotten so big. Most of their eight children are married and some already have children of their own. We hug and kiss one another and wish we had a table large enough for all the Libeskinds and Gomolinskis to be together on this joyous holiday.

When they leave, we stand around our table. There are nine of us: Mama and Tatte; my brothers, Josek, Idek, and Beniek; my nephew, two-year-old Marek; my sisters, Regina and Hela; and me. Sadly missing is Hela's husband, Jacob, who is in the Polish army somewhere on the eastern border.

It is sundown and Mama says the blessing as she lights the candles. Tatte says the prayer over the wine and we each take our first sip. Then Tatte says the blessing over the *karpas* as we dip it in the salt water to remember the tears of our ancestors. Tatte holds up a *matzo*. There are three *matzot* under a cloth on the *matzo* plate and the middle one, which he holds up, is called the *afikomen*—the dessert.

Tatte takes it into another room to hide it, but this year we are missing the excitement of little children rushing off to search for it later in the Seder. Who will find it and get a special prize? Regina is too old and Marek too young to care, and this year there's more reason for worry than joy.

Now it is time for the Four Questions. I still remember my pride when I was six and the youngest who could read. It was my job to ask the Four Questions. Now Regina, at twelve, is the youngest who can read. It is not exciting for her anymore, but she does a good job. She sings them in Hebrew and then reads them again in Yiddish. "Why is this night different from all other nights? On all other nights we eat both leavened and unleavened bread. Why on this night do we eat only unleavened bread? On all other nights we eat all kinds of herbs. Why on this night do we eat especially bitter herbs? On all other nights we do not usually dip our foods even once. Why on this night do we dip them twice? On all other nights we eat while sitting up straight. Why on this night only do we recline?"

And Tatte answers the questions. He explains that we eat the *matzo* like the flat bread of our ancestors, who had no time to let their bread rise in their sudden flight from Egypt; that the bitter herbs recall our bitter lives there as slaves, and the salt water we dip them in symbolizes our tears. He says we are all free like kings, now, so we can eat like kings and recline.

Then we all take turns reading the story from the Haggadah.

Mama begins: "People have risen up to destroy us but the Holy One, blessed be God, delivers us from their hands. Our story begins with bondage and degradation but ends with freedom and dignity."

Josek gets to read the part about the famine in Israel and how Jacob took his people into Egypt, where they became great and strong.

Then Idek reads that Pharaoh feared the Israelites and made them slaves. The Jews cried to God. He revealed himself to Moses in the Burning Bush and told him to go to Pharaoh as His messenger and tell Pharaoh to "Let my people go." When Pharaoh refused, God sent the first plague; and with each refusal, another plague; until after the ninth refusal, He sent the worst plague of all.

Idek continues to read that in preparation for their flight, God had Moses instruct the Jews that on the tenth of that month they must take a perfect, unblemished male lamb or goat into their home, keep it for four days, and then, together as an assembly, each household must kill their animal at twilight, and smear some of the blood on the doorposts and window frames of their homes. Then they were to roast the animal over a fire and eat it quickly and bake their bread unleavened, as there would be too little time to wait for the dough to rise. They must be dressed with their sandals on and be prepared to flee.

Now it is Hela who leads us in reciting the Ten Plagues. With each one, we dip our pinkie fingers into our wineglasses and shake a drop onto our white china plates. It definitely looks like blood. In a deep voice Hela chants in Hebrew: blood, frogs, lice, insects, cattle disease, boils, hail, locusts, darkness. Then God sends the last plague: the death of the firstborn sons of Egypt.

Beniek continues the story. Because God had instructed us to mark our houses with the lambs' blood, the Angel of Death knew which homes were Jewish and passed them by; our firstborn sons were spared but the oldest son born to any Egyptian family perished.

At this part, Hela grabs Marek and holds him tightly to her breast. Beniek reads that when Pharaoh's own son died, his agony was more than even he could endure. Pharaoh surrendered to God's greater power and finally agreed to let the Israelites go.

Moses led the Jews quickly out of Egypt, taking what little they could carry and their flat, unrisen bread. When they reached the Red Sea, the waters miraculously parted to allow the Israelites to walk across. But when the Egyptians, running close behind, tried to follow, the sea flooded over them, drowning them all.

It is now my turn to finish the Passover story before the dinner. I read of how Moses and the Jews wandered in the Sinai Desert. When they reached Mount Sinai, God instructed Moses to climb alone to the top and there He revealed to him the Ten Commandments and our laws and covenant with Him, the Torah. And then I lead the song "Dayenu," which translates as "It Would Have Been Enough for Us": "God has done so many wonderful things for us. If he had only brought us out of Egypt, *dayenu*. If he had only given us the Sabbath, *dayenu*. If he had only given us the Torah, *dayenu*."

We sing and sing: "Dye, dye-AI-nu, dye, dye-AI-nu, dye, dye-AI-nu, dye-AI-nu, dye-ai-NU, dye-ai-nu . . ."

And then we drink from our second cup of wine.

We look at the Seder tray and Mama reads about the meaning of the lamb bone and the *matzo*. Tatte blesses the *matzo* and explains why we have the *maror*, the bitter herb. At long last, we can put the *charoset* on the *matzo*, like the mortar our ancestors put on the bricks when they were slaves in Egypt, and we eat.

What a feast! First, we have hard-boiled eggs in salt water, then the *matzo*-ball soup, then roast chicken with the most delicious *matzo*-meal stuffing, always moist and juicy because of the chicken fat—the *schmaltz*. We also have beef brisket and candied carrots, hot apricot-and-prune fruit compote, and a sweet *matzo kugel*. And coconut macaroons and sponge cake for dessert.

But I cannot stop hearing the song "Dayenu." It is ringing in my ears, haunting me. Maybe it is the wine. The tune won't leave my head, but now I'm hearing different, horrifying words. I'm thinking that when Hitler became führer of Germany, *dayenu*, that would have been enough. When the anti-Semitic Nuremberg laws were passed, *dayenu*.

The song is drumming a beat in my brain. Just last year, Hitler took over the country of Austria and all his anti-Jewish laws applied there. Then Jews in Germany and Austria had to register all their property. In September, Great Britain and France agreed to give Germany the Sudetenland. That's part of Czechoslovakia, so close to our western Polish border. *Dayenu*.

We all feared what was coming. We knew. This was more than enough. Now all Jews in Germany and Austria and the Sudetenland have to have a *J* stamped on their identity papers. Last October, Germany expelled seventeen thousand Polish Jews who had been living in Germany and, at first, the Poles refused to let them into Poland. They were stranded on the border for weeks. *Dayenu*.

We were shocked, but sadly not surprised, by the violent anti-Jewish pogroms that were carried out last November 9 and 10. Every single city and village that had Jews in Germany, Austria, and the Sudetenland was affected. It was called Kristallnacht, the Night of Broken Glass. Over one thousand synagogues were burned and destroyed, tens of thousands of Jewish shops and homes were vandalized, thirty thousand Jewish men and boys were sent to concentration camps, ninety-one people were killed, and a law was passed stating that all Jews must transfer their retail businesses to Germans. *Dayenu.* Enough.

But it still wasn't enough. On November 15, all Jewish students were expelled from German schools. And one month after Kristallnacht, Hitler told the Jews they owed Germany one billion German marks to repair the damages of Kristallnacht!

It is hard to believe that the Jews paid for what the Nazis did. But what else could they do? They had no choice.

In January, exactly six years to the day after Hitler became chancellor of Germany, Heniek and I heard him speaking on the radio. Hitler was at the Reichstag, the parliament building in Berlin. He said that if there were going to be a war, it would mean the *Vernichtung*—the annihilation—of all the European Jews. Heniek and I sat there and hugged each other, shaking and feeling sick.

And just two weeks ago, in March, the Germans marched into Czechoslovakia and now they occupy that country, which borders Poland. It is more than enough.

As I sit with my family around the Passover table at this annual celebration of our freedom, I wonder: Where is our God? Dinner is over and we sing more songs. We open the door for Elijah. We drink from our cups of wine. Regina finds the *afikomen* and we sing the song "Chad Gadya," and again I fear that our past is becoming our future. The words of "Chad Gadya" ("One Little Goat") are:

My father bought a little goat for two coins,
but a cat came and ate the goat
and the dog came and killed the cat
and the stick came and beat the dog
and the fire came and burned the stick
and the water came and put out the fire
and the ox came to drink the water
but the butcher came to kill the ox
and then the Angel of Death came to kill the butcher,
but then God killed the Angel of Death.

And I think: We Jews have been so patient through five thousand years of so much pain and terror, always fervently depending on God to save us. And He always has, but after so much suffering. I wonder: What will happen to us Polish Jews? How long must we wait before God comes to kill the Angel of Death, and what will happen in the meantime?

Wojna!

War is the national industry of Prussia.
—Honoré-Gabriel Riqueti, Count of Mirabeau (1749–1791)

SEPTEMBER 1, 1939

It's eight in the morning and I should start packing to go back to the university in Warsaw, but it's already very hot and it is the last Friday of my vacation, which I want to savor. Soon it will be Shabbos, so I decide to wait until Sunday to pack. On Tuesday, Heniek and I will take the train to Warsaw together. He has a good job apprenticing for a lawyer. I will be starting my third year of university. The summer was lovely and lazy, but I am excited to get back into learning, especially because I will be studying Shakespeare and Charles Dickens and the Victorian period of literature and art.

By this time, I feel adept at reading and writing in English and have fallen in love with the language and the literature. There is something musical about English. I no longer love hearing German spoken, and now when Heniek and I listen to the German radio, the sounds of the words are as ugly to my ears as the dark and frightening things they are saying.

We know that since Hitler occupied Czechoslovakia in March, he has been massing Nazi troops near the western Polish border. In August, the Molotov-Ribbentrop Pact was signed by Germany and the Soviet Union. They called it a nonaggression treaty, but we know what it really means. In case of war, Germany and the Soviets will divide Poland between them. So we are not safe on our western border with the Germans ready to invade, and we are not safe on the eastern border where the Russians will come in. We keep hearing of the Germans' need for *Lebensraum*. Again and again Hitler screams that the Germans need more room for their perfect Aryan people. We know that Poland is a large, beautiful country and conveniently just next door. We know that Hitler sees the Poles as *Untermenschen*, subhuman creatures. If the Nazis view the Poles as *Untermenschen*, what are we Jews? I shiver to think about that.

We have enough virulent anti-Semitism in Poland, we don't need more from the Germans. It was always there, of course, but it started getting much worse five years ago. First, the Polish government tried to restrict the way we Jews killed our animals; our kosher laws caused cruelty to animals, they said. My father was incensed because the way the *shochet* (the ritual slaughterer) slits the jugular vein of the animal is much more humane than the way the Poles keep hitting their poor animals over the head.

More and more, there is terrible, hateful graffiti—*Christ killers* and *Death to all Zhids*—scrawled on some of our Jewish buildings. Just last Christmas and Easter, the rabbi's son Tulek Lau and my cousin Janek warned us to stay home and off the streets for fear of attacks. Janek also warned my brothers, Josek and Beniek and Idek, to stop playing soccer in the park on Sundays. He said when the local Polish soccer team loses the weekly game with their opponents from another town, they work out their anger by beating up Jews. When they win, they celebrate by beating up Jews. Even though I hate any thought of violence, I must admit having felt some pride when one Sunday, a year ago, some of our Jewish boys, including my brother-in-law, Jacob Brem, and his friend Leon Reichmann, went after the Polish boys and beat them up first.

Last year, in 1938, the old lies about Jews killing Christian children were being circulated in Piotrków, just as those hateful lies had been spewed out in the Middle Ages and in Spain during the Inquisition in the fifteenth century.

Just this July, after the Lau family returned from their summer vacation in Rabka, Tulek told Regina two chilling stories. Tulek and Milek and their friends had been playing a game they often played when they were in the countryside. A few of the boys would jump on the back of a farmer's cart, and when the farmer saw them, they would jump off. But this time, one driver screamed at them: "Just wait, Hitler is on his way, and he will finish you!" And then Tulek told Regina that the train the Laus rode as they returned to Piotrków took four hours longer than usual because so many uniformed young men kept boarding the train: Polish soldiers being sent to the western front.

Suddenly, Rebbitzin Lau knocks at our door. A look of horror is on her face. "Tulek has just run home. He was with his friends at the corner of Jerozolimska and Piłsudskiego Streets. They heard a loud siren and saw two trucks full of Polish soldiers driving fast down the street, and the soldiers were shouting 'Wojna!'" she says. "Turn on your radio, Gucia."

A chill runs through me—*wojna* means *war*.

And through the static we hear the news. It has come. The Germans have invaded Poland.

I feel a perverse momentary thrill: something extraordinary is about to break the tedium of everyday life. But immediately, as the true meaning of the words on the radio sinks in, my excitement turns to fear.

All day and all night we hear people going up and down the stairs to the rabbi's apartment. We suppose they are asking for information and advice. From Hela's balcony we see truck after truck of Polish soldiers hurrying west to the border near Wieluń. Mama and Tatte are afraid the war might come to Piotrków immediately—this very day. They hurry off to both butcher stores hoping to sell all the meat to people brave enough to leave their houses and clever enough to stock up for the storm that is coming our way. Tatte decides not to order any more meat for the time being, and by sundown both stores are completely sold out. Mama comes home early and Tatte stays to close and shutter both shops before he rushes home. He feels the safest thing for us to do is to quickly leave Piotrków for a while and go to the countryside, where we know a Polish farmer.

Like everyone in Piotrków we leave our lights off after dark; a protective blackout in case the German air force is looking for bombing targets. We eat a sad and quiet Shabbos dinner by the light of the Shabbos candles. It is too dark to get ready to leave. We feel that God will forgive us for packing and leaving on Shabbos. Judas Maccabeus told his men that "the Sabbath is holy, but life is holier."

September 2–3, 1939

We are so surprised. It has been very quiet all night. Perhaps the Polish soldiers are fighting more fiercely than we had supposed and are successfully defending our border. Nevertheless, we get up early on Shabbos and pack some bedding. We carefully put my great-grandmother's silver Shabbos candlesticks and a silver Shabbos *kiddush* cup in the middle of the bedding. We don't take a lot of clothes because we plan to return soon. Mama has a beautiful engagement ring of platinum with a sparkling diamond and she sews it into the hem of her coat.

Tatte leaves the apartment to get our horse and carriage. I have no time to talk to Heniek because we have so much work to do, and that makes me frantic. I have time to write him only a few desperate words in our urgency to flee. I say that we may never see each other again and that I will love him forever. I ask Rebbitzin Lau to give it to him.

When I hug and kiss the rebbitzin goodbye she says the rabbi has decided that his place is to stay with his congregation and that he will even hold Shabbos services as usual in the Great Synagogue. She tells me that all day Friday, when people asked him what to do, he would quote Isaiah 26:20: "Hide but a little moment, until the indignation passes." We all feel frightened and empty and numb. Will the indignation truly pass? And if it will pass, when will that be? We are almost in a trance.

Tatte comes to the back with the carriage and my mother is in tears. She is worrying about her dear brother, my uncle Josef, and Tante Sura and all of our cousins: Janek, Mania and David Tanenbaum, Hancia, Mendel and Genia and their baby Shlomo, Moshe, Chaim and Rebekah, Mala and Rozia.

We quickly squeeze tightly into the carriage: Hela and Marek, Regina, Josek, Beniek, Idek, me, Mama, Tatte, and of course Janova. Although the day is warm, I feel icy cold and somewhat detached as our carriage heads down the busy streets. I feel that I am merely watching a movie and that there is a woman in that carriage named Gucia, but she is not me.

We have made this same trip every summer for as long as I can remember, but in a very different movie. Every year after Passover my parents would take a train to the village of Przyglow and arrange to rent a peasant's cottage for July and August. Then, as soon as our schools closed, the maids would take us to Przyglow in a carriage with all our clothes and kosher kitchen equipment. My parents would come by train every weekend. Since Polish law forbids the opening of any business on Sundays, they didn't have to worry about the butcher stores and could come on Friday before sundown and return Sunday night.

In those lovely summers of the past, we spent our days playing in the fields, gazing at the sheep, swimming in the river, going for hikes, reading, and visiting with friends. The peasants were poor and grateful for the extra money from renting their house to us. They would simply sleep and cook outside. It was so warm in the summer, it didn't seem to be a hardship for them. But this trip to Przyglow has absolutely no similarity to those of my happy childhood.

Piłsudskiego Street is mobbed with people, a few in carriages, but mostly on foot, Jews and Poles, frantically pushing carts filled with their valuables, heading the same way we are, southeast, away from the Germans.

Just as we are nearing the outskirts of Piotrków, we hear and see German airplanes above, and the bombs start falling on our beloved city. The noise is deafening, and the sudden explosions, fires, and smoke fill us all with terror. The horse rears up and then gallops faster and faster, and we are soon away from the noise and smoke. I am trembling as I imagine what is happening to Heniek, my relatives, the Laus, and Piotrków.

It takes us only an hour to get to our cottage in Przyglow, and the farmer is not surprised to see us. He, too, has heard about the German invasion and thought we might be coming for safety. It is almost like a typical summer except we are so frightened. We put our bedding down on the floors of the little cottage and have a very light meal of bread and cold leftover chicken from Friday night's dinner.

Sunday morning, Tatte and Mama look at a map and decide we must hurry farther southeast to get away from the Germans. We will go to Sulejow. We load everything back into the carriages and start out, but suddenly we hear planes above us and then see bombs falling behind us and in front of us. We are in the middle of a cloud of dark, acrid smoke and deafening thunder.

The road is full of Polish soldiers coming our way. They are running away from the Germans. We must face the truth. Poland is lost. It's too late. We are surrounded. There is no way out. We turn around and go back home to the smoke and noise and frightened, scurrying people of Piotrków and our unknown future.

SEPTEMBER 4, 1939

We are home. The bombs have spared us and 21 Piłsudskiego is still standing, with all the windows still in their frames. We are numb and frightened and have no idea what will happen next. Our building is half-empty. Because we have no cellar, many of our tenants fled to other buildings nearby for refuge from the bombing. But now the bombing seems to have stopped. It feels eerily quiet, although we can hear distant explosions, almost like thunder, coming from the south. There are rumors that the Germans are coming on foot. I have had no word from Heniek but I keep that to myself. Hela has had no word from Jacob for three months.

SEPTEMBER 5, 1939

Today feels almost like a normal day. It is quiet and Koenigstein's Bakery down the street at number 9 is open, so we can have fresh bread.

A note from Heniek arrives. It simply says that he is well and loves me and would rather be holding my hand on a train to Warsaw than huddling in a cellar with his family.

At two p.m. our family sits around the dining room table for dinner, as if all is normal. My mother and father talk about ordering meat to-morrow and opening the butcher shops on Thursday, assuming things stay quiet. Soon it will be the Jewish New Year, the High Holidays, ten days of prayer and atonement and commitment to *tikkun olam* and a better future.

But around four o'clock, we hear loud gunfire very close to our house. We all run to Hela's apartment and look out the balcony. There are about a hundred three-wheeled motorcycles with little carts on the sides, each driver and passenger a German soldier. Their uniforms are greenish and they have round steel helmets on their heads and they all wear that frightening Nazi symbol, the black swastika on a bloodred armband. So that's why the bombing has stopped. The Germans have entered our city. The sound of exploding bombs has been replaced by the noise of gunfire. The soldiers are shooting into the apartments just across the street at 17 Piłsudskiego. One of the tenants must have made the mistake of peeping out of the doorway, because he now lies in a spreading pool of what looks like beet borscht. We run back to our apartment, close all the windows and shutters, and try to pray to God.

SEPTEMBER 6, 1939

We hear distant gunfire all morning but Piłsudskiego Street seems quiet. Late in the afternoon the Laus come back and the rebbitzin comes to see us. She is shaking and her nose and eyes are red. The weather is stifling hot but her hands are like ice. We give her some hot tea and milk and what we have left of the coffee cake. In a trembling voice she tells us that since midnight on Saturday her family had been crowded in with about forty others a few blocks away in the cellar of the Radoshitz rabbi, Rabbi Finkler. That morning a number of military vehicles pulled up outside the house and soldiers poured out. They surrounded the exclusively Jewish block nearby, bounded by Zamkowa, Wspolna, Starowarzawska, and Jerozolimska Streets, and fired into the houses. As the tenants ran out, fleeing in every direction, the Germans kept shooting into the buildings. The buildings were then set on fire and the entire block burned down. By the end, six Jews were dead and twenty injured.

Then she quietly tells us that on Monday the Germans bombed Sulejow. There are thousands of refugees and casualties, Polish and Jewish, and hundreds of people from Piotrków have been killed. Sulejow! That is where we were planning to go to escape the Germans.

My whole body feels as icy as the rebbitzin's hands. She says she must get back to her family and she leaves. The tea is untouched. The coffee cake sits with every crumb intact.

SEPTEMBER 7, 1939

The Nazis are now suddenly, brutally, in charge of our city, our country, and our lives. They have set up loudspeakers all over our neighborhood and are constantly shouting into them, barking out orders, informing us that there is now a curfew from six at night till dawn. They are emphatic that they will shoot anyone who violates this curfew right there on the spot. They also scream and shout that although Poles are subhuman, Jews are less than that, and therefore Poles may no longer work for or serve Jews.

Bolek, the janitor, has already fled Piotrków and gone to his family in the countryside. The Nazis have come and taken our horse and carriage and Wojcek has been forced to leave, as well. Janova, who is practically Regina's second mother, must leave us tonight. Janova is an orphan, and has absolutely no family or place to go. She will try to find Krysia, who lives near Łódź, twenty-six kilometers away.

Janova hopes to be able to get on the train, but we are all frightened for her, and sad for ourselves. She has been such a major part of our family and has always done all the housekeeping. What shall we do without her? And how will she survive without us? Mama gives Janova a nice dress and a coat of Hela's to take. She would have given more, but knowing the desperate struggle of Jews in Germany simply to survive, Mama worries about depleting our resources. We are all desolate. Mama, Hela, and Regina are sobbing and making everyone's shoulders wet.

SEPTEMBER 8, 1939

The bombing and shooting seem to be over. We are running low on food and so I have volunteered to go out to the bakery and vegetable stores. We will not allow Mama to take the risk. She is too valuable to our family. Hela has Marek to take care of and Regina is just thirteen. My brothers and father dare not go outside the house. It is safer for a woman to go. We hear that men are being beaten, arrested, or shot.

I stand in a very long line of Poles and Jews, all women, and my ears are buzzing with snatches of horrible bits of gossip and rumors in Polish and Yiddish. God forbid that they be true. A woman turns to me and asks if I have heard about Baila Reichmann's youngest son, Abraham. He was shot and killed last night for being on the street after the six-o'clock curfew. Abraham was only twenty-three. Poor Pani Reichmann. She's been a widow since her husband, Hercka, died just after Abraham was born, leaving her with six young children under age eleven. For over twenty years she has carried the full burden of the family's wholesale hardware and building supply store. With the help of her three sons, each leaving school as a young teenager to work in the business, she'd made it a big success. Now, with her oldest son, Josek, studying in Jerusalem, she must grieve for her youngest, leaving only Leon to help run the business and for her to lean on at home.

And then another woman whispers to the women around me, in Yiddish. Have we heard that the Nazis took three girls away this morning? She names three of my former classmates. These girls were very attractive and had reputations for being a bit "wild." The Germans just grabbed them off the street and pushed them into a green Volkswagen and drove off. The women start gossiping about why the Nazis would take these beautiful young girls and what will happen to them. My stomach tightens and churns.

By the time I get to the head of the line my hunger is replaced by nausea. There is very little food left. I am lucky to get the last day-old *challah*, a few pounds of potatoes, two wilted cabbages, and ten old, wrinkled carrots. With Janova gone, we will all have to pitch in. I guess Mama and Hela will cook the meals. The only thing I have ever cooked before is coffee and that was a disaster.

SEPTEMBER 9, 1939

We are just about to sit down for our Shabbos dinner. With only a few potatoes, cabbage, and old carrots, our meal of watery soup does not look very appetizing. We hear heavy boots coming up the stairs. Regina peeks out the door and comes back crying. There are two large men in German uniforms pounding impatiently on the rabbi's door. We cannot eat a bite. We sit there listening for more steps. After an hour we hear the rabbi's door open and loud footsteps going down the stairs. Regina again peeks out our door and sees that the two Germans are leaving alone. Mama rushes to talk to the rebbitzin, who says that, surprisingly, it was a very nice, polite meeting. Rabbi Lau had been summoned to go immediately to the office of the new military governor of Piotrków, Colonel Brandt. When the rabbi said that it was his Sabbath and he could do no work, the Nazis said that Sunday was their Sabbath and they could do no work, so the rabbi was to show up at their office on Monday. We all feel greatly relieved, and a bit of hope is kindled. We even try a taste of the now-cold soup and the dry, stale bread.

SEPTEMBER 11–12, 1939

On Monday, when Rabbi Lau comes back from the meeting with the new military governor, he says that Colonel Brandt complimented him on his perfect German. The colonel was very polite but emphatic that no Jews were to show any resistance whatsoever to any of the commands of the Nazis. He further declared that the rabbi must provide two hundred strong men each day to work for the Nazis to ensure the peace and to take care of necessary city tasks. The rabbi explained that he was just the spiritual leader of the people, the leader of the Jewish Court, and that it was the responsibility of the Community Council to handle relations between the people and the government. Only the council had access to the population rolls, and until it resumed functioning, there would be no way to implement the colonel's order.

On Tuesday, we hear a rumor that Polish police and German soldiers have started going house to house forcibly taking strong young men for the German labor needs. We are so frightened for Josek, Idek, and Beniek, and try to think of some way to make a hiding place for them, but we have no cellar or attic. Our minds are totally empty. Our heads feel full of cotton. We feel paralyzed and cannot think or plan. We are consumed by fear and dread. This cannot really be happening.

SEPTEMBER 13, 1939

It is the start of the High Holidays, with Rosh Hashanah beginning at sundown. On this day, three men in black uniforms with red swastika armbands come to Rabbi Lau's. They introduce themselves as Radom District Security Police and, again speaking politely, tell him that they are now in charge of dealings with the Jews and repeat Colonel Brandt's demand for Jewish workers. Also, the rabbi is to provide without delay a lot of information about the Jews of Piotrków: a map showing where they live, names, addresses, properties, community organizations, names of officers, tax rolls, etc.

Rabbi Lau tells the police that as soon as Rosh Hashanah is over, he will contact Mendel Wajshof, Heniek's father, who is secretary of the Community Council. But right now he is required to lead his congregation in celebrating this sacred holiday.

The rabbi then takes the opportunity to ask permission of the Germans to hold services at the Great Synagogue that evening and for the next two days.

"Of course," they say, glancing at each other. "No one will disturb your prayers."

Then they remind him, again ever so politely, as though as a courtesy, about the six p.m. to six a.m. curfew, making the evening service impossible. For the first time in our lives, we don't go to *shul* that evening for Rosh Hashanah services, nor do we go, after the end of curfew, for the morning service. Rebbitzin Lau says that only about thirty people were brave enough or devoted enough to be there that morning.

Thursday, after the morning services, the Germans come again and tell the rabbi that now they need one thousand workers every day, and if the Community Council does not gather the men, then the Nazis will, and we know it will mean brutal beatings and killings.

That afternoon, some Jewish men come to the rabbi to tell him they have seen piles of wood stacked up against the walls of the Great Synagogue and to ask should they try to remove the sacred Torah scrolls and other holy things before the Nazis burn the synagogue down. Rabbi Lau has already been summoned to meet with the new German mayor, Hans Drecksel. He says he will try to find out what the Germans have planned for the synagogue.

When the rabbi learns the purpose of the meeting he is rendered speechless. Drecksel demands that the Jews pay the Nazis twenty-five thousand Polish *zlotys* for the damages caused in the first days of the German occupation. This is the same extortion as when the Germans made the Jews pay for all the damages the Germans did during Kristallnacht. We will need a miracle to find all that money and, sadly, it seems that God and the prophets and the possibility of miracles are now very far away. The rabbi collects himself and tries to bring up the issue of the synagogue but Drecksel directs him back to Colonel Brandt at Wehrmacht headquarters.

Once he's sitting across from Brandt, Rabbi Lau proposes that perhaps the Jews could be helpful by emptying out all the furniture and decorations from the synagogue, and then the Germans could use the building as a prison for all the Polish prisoners of war who are being kept in makeshift camps outside of the city. The colonel laughs and says that that was exactly his plan and that he had stacked up wood against the building so that we Jews could make the latrines for the prisoners. Latrines in our Great Synagogue! An exquisite synagogue built in 1791; famous, admired, and respected throughout all of Poland. Latrines!

That night a group of brave and devoted young men organized by Tulek Lau take as many of the Torah scrolls, candlesticks, and other sacred books and objects as they can carry out of the synagogue, put them into coffins, and bury them in the Jewish cemetery. Thank God no one found them breaking the curfew or saw what they were doing.

As soon as this horror is over they will be able to dig them up. For now our most sacred objects are safe.

And the next day, Heniek comes to my house. What a joy and relief to actually see him and hug him and talk to him. We hold each other for a long time and some of my numbness disappears. He asks me to help him and his father and the Community Council to compile a list of all the Jews in Piotrków, their names, addresses, and properties. This won't be a difficult task because the community has always been a city within the city. For centuries we Jews had our own census and tax records. It was compulsory that all Jews pay taxes to the Community Council, which in turn paid for the maintenance of the synagogues, the rabbis' and cantors' salaries and living expenses, the upkeep of the cemetery, the Jewish orphanage, and the Benevolent Societies. We have always taken care of our own because no one else would take care of us.

Pan Wajshof and some other men, Heniek, and I work the whole night into the next day copying down for the Germans all the information about the twenty thousand Jews of Piotrków.

As I am copying I am thinking, What are you doing, Gucia? You are collaborating with this evil enemy.

By dawn, even though I love and respect Heniek and want to help his father as much as I can, I decide I will not do this again.

Tatte wants to open the butcher stores but Mama begs him to wait one more week. The days become endless, melting into each other with new horrors and rumors. We all begin to lose track of the time. At some point between Rosh Hashanah and Yom Kippur, the Nazis come to our apartment building and drag out four tenants from the third floor. The men are returned the next day horribly beaten. We, and they, have no idea why they were taken and treated so brutally, but, thank God, they were returned and they are alive.

Each day I stand in line hoping to find potatoes and bread to buy.

Yesterday an older woman in front of me started sobbing and wailing. She asked if we had heard the news. On the second day of Rosh Hashanah, some Germans had gone to a small Hasidic synagogue and had forced, at gunpoint, about twenty-five of those most devout, older Jews out of the synagogue. They were pushed into trucks, defiling this sacred holiday by riding in a vehicle, and then the old Jews were forced to go to the public toilets and clean them with their prayer shawls. Another woman said she had heard that some of the Nazis have been tearing the beards and *peyos* (side curls) off the old Jews, leaving them in agony, the skin of their faces in shreds, dripping blood. Another woman moaned about how the Germans came and shot the *mezuzah* (small decorative scroll containing Torah excerpts) off her door. How convenient for the Germans that by obeying the biblical command to affix these sacred markers to our doorposts, we make their job of finding us easier. I am praying that these are just *bubbe meises*, old wives' tales. I cannot yet believe that humans can do this to each other.

Tatte has decided to reopen the stores. First he has to go find out if the man who sells the cows is still in business and if the *shochet* is still there to slaughter the cows in the kosher manner. He also has to see if the two stores have had any damage from the bombs. It is hard to do this without Wojcek and the horse and carriage, but somehow Tatte is successful and he comes home happier than we have seen him since September 1.

Everything is in order. He has bought a cow and it has been slaughtered. He has had the front part of the cow delivered to the kosher store for Mama and the back part of the cow to the non-kosher store for him. They will reopen the stores in the morning.

The clock tells us the time, but like in a bad dream, the days no longer have a beginning or end. We drift through each nameless day.

It is two p.m. and we are sitting down to a dinner of watery potato soup with a little bit of meat and bones from the butcher store. The bread is very bad. The baker apologized. There is no way to get white flour anymore and he is doing the best he can. But this black coarse bread makes us want to gag.

Suddenly we hear what sounds like a train rushing up our stairs, and the crystal chandelier sways and clinks noisily over the dining room table. There is a loud pounding on our front door and loud rough German voices screaming, "*Schnell! Schnell!* Open the door now!"

Beniek and Josek and Idek rush into the bedroom and close the door. Hela grabs Marek, holding him tightly, and Regina goes to the door. Five men in black uniforms with red swastika armbands rush into the room, guns pointing at us.

We do not move. We do not breathe. We look at our bowls of watery soup.

They grab all the silverware from our places and stuff it in a large bag. They rush to the breakfront and open the drawers and find the rest of the silverware. They toss our sterling silver tea and coffee service, which is on top of the breakfront, into another large bag. It was my parents' wedding gift from Uncle Josef and Tante Sura. They storm into the library and the bedrooms, not even noticing my brothers. They do not want Jews right now, just Jewish property. Seeing my *tatte*'s special, favorite chair, a beautiful carved mahogany armchair upholstered in a rich royal blue Belgian velvet, two of the soldiers lift and carry it out the door and down the stairs. These Nazis are animals but they do have good taste.

The others follow with their filled bags and slam the door.

I don't think any of us has breathed. I am outraged yet helpless.

They have guns and power and we have watery potato soup and dry black bread. Mama bursts into tears of relief and hysterical laughter.

She had hidden her grandmother's silver Shabbos candlesticks in the laundry basket and they are still safe, buried in the dirty clothes. Those candlesticks are the most precious property we have and so we feel that we have triumphed over the Nazis. This time.

SEPTEMBER 25, 1939

Rebbitzin Lau comes to tell us that the rabbi has just returned from a very disturbing meeting with Mayor Drecksel. Today was the deadline to deliver the twenty-five thousand *zlotys* demanded. The rabbi and the Community Council had done what they could to raise the money, and the rabbi carried a briefcase filled with donated jewels, gold, and cash from the Jews who could help. It was far from twenty-five thousand *zlotys*, but the mayor seemed pleased. Rabbi Lau then asked the mayor if the curfew could be shortened and could something be done to better protect Jewish public institutions and people. The mayor thought this was a wonderful idea and said that he thought this could be best achieved by forming a *Jüdisches Wohnviertel* (Jewish residential district), that all the Jews of Piotrków would move to one area of the city—for their safety and protection.

The rabbi is very frightened. The mayor is suggesting the establishment of a ghetto.

The Ghetto

Ghettos in the various cities were not all organized at the same time, but at different periods. Venice and Salerno had ghettos in the eleventh century, and Prague is said to have had one as early as the tenth. There were ghettos in Italy, Bohemia, Moravia, Austria, Hungary, Germany, Poland, and Turkey. They were chiefly an outcome of intolerance, and oppressive conditions were often added to compulsory residence within the ghetto . . . The French Revolution (1789), which proclaimed the principle of freedom and equality, first shook the foundations of the ghetto, and the general uprising of 1848 throughout Europe finally swept away this remnant of medieval intolerance. In the whole civilized world there is now not a single ghetto, in the original meaning of the word.
—The Jewish Encyclopedia, 1906

OCTOBER 8, 1939

Less than two weeks after the meeting with Mayor Drecksel, what the rabbi feared comes to pass. Piotrków has the dubious distinction of being named the first ghetto in the German-occupied territory. As part of this new order, Mayor Drecksel establishes the *Aeltestenrat* (Council of Elders), or as we call it, the *Judenrat* (Jewish Council).

Everyone is afraid of what this means, but then we are more hopeful when we learn who is on it. Drecksel appoints twelve members from our Community Council, including the rabbi, but to his relief, not Heniek's father. And on October 28 it is official. The Germans have marked off the boundaries of the ghetto with bluish-gray signposts. On each is the word *ghetto*. Above the letters are a skull and crossbones.

Zalman Tannenberg is appointed chairman of the *Judenrat*. He turns out to be an able leader and often finds a way to circumvent the worst of the Nazis' edicts, so we start to feel a little less tense about it. But then we feel betrayed when he makes an unthinkable decision. He sets up a Jewish police force (*Jüdischer Ordnungsdienst*), Jews to oversee other Jews, responsible to the Germans. We are afraid it will become a tool for the Nazis to use against us. Who are these people who would volunteer to collaborate with the enemy? I suppose they are just humans who want to protect themselves and their families. Maybe they think they can help us with the Nazis. In protest, the rabbi resigns from the *Judenrat*.

We learn from Heniek that the cities of Łódź and Kalisz have been officially designated as parts of the Third Reich, meaning that they will soon be *Judenrein*—clean of Jews. Soon no Jews will be permitted to live there anymore. Jews would pollute the city. All their property will be seized.

The next day Heniek comes with more news. Piotrków is designated part of the General Government. We are under German administration, but we are not annexed as part of the Third Reich, and so we are more independent. That means Jews can live here and, I guess, our pollution of Piotrków is fine.

Tatte and Mama come home ashen and shaking. Mama is in tears and Tatte looks as if he might cry, too. Some Nazis had come to the non-kosher shop and told him it was now officially closed. Just like that. They took away all the meat in a truck and smashed the front windows and the glass of all the counters. Tatte rushed as quickly as he could to the kosher butcher shop and got there just in time to be with Mama when the Nazis came. We are horrified, but we thank God that our parents are alive and unhurt.

Although Heniek's father is not a member of the *Judenrat*, he is committed to *tikkun olam* and still feels a moral and civic duty to continue working on behalf of the community. He and his colleagues are trying to help find housing for all the Jews who are escaping from Łódź and Kalisz. It doesn't matter if they own properties or businesses. They must surrender everything to the Reich. So many are fleeing with whatever possessions they can fit in a single cart or on their backs. Everything left behind will automatically become the property of the Germans and the Poles. Well, maybe Krysia and Janova will benefit from these Jewish losses. As I learned in first grade, sometimes one person's misfortune is another's good luck.

Łódź is only twenty-six kilometers away, so some people will start arriving as soon as tomorrow. Rebbitzin Lau is already clearing out her dining room for our relatives from Kalisz to move into. It has a door opening directly onto the hallway, so the Laus can close off the other door from the rest of their apartment and at least the two families will have some privacy. But I can't imagine all seven of them in one room. There's Mama's brother Mendel Libeskind and my aunt Sprintza; their son Elkanah, his wife, Dora, and their child; and their oldest daughter, Hinda, and her husband. I guess they'll have to share our toilet or use the outhouse. The rebbitzin stays calm as usual, so positive and practical and comforting. She says how lucky we are that our apartment building is within the ghetto boundaries and that none of us will have to move. She is right. It could be far worse. All Piotrków Jews who live outside the boundaries of the ghetto must leave everything they have, just like the people from Łódź and Kalisz, and move into the ghetto. I suppose it comes naturally to Chaya Lau, after all her years as the rabbi's wife, to help people keep their spirits up. But I wonder what the rebbitzin really thinks and feels deep down, in her private heart and soul.

I remember how in happier times we always looked forward to visits from Mendel and Sprintza because they were so much fun. Mendel never had much to say, but that was a good thing because Sprintza had more than enough for both of them. She was a little dynamo, a real force of nature, short and fat, not even as tall as Regina, who was only ten the last time they came. Sprintza took over every room she entered, but no one minded, not even Mama, because Sprintza was so good-natured and funny.

I love to laugh and can overlook a lot if someone is funny. Heniek's wit is what made me fall in love with him. Making people laugh has never been my talent, at least not on purpose. But sometimes I can be funny by accident. After Mendel and Sprintza's last visit I was telling Heniek that Mendel is afraid of Sprintza. He asked me how could I tell and I answered, "When Sprintza speaks, Mendel trembles." This cracked him up, which then cracked me up. He said the words sounded almost biblical, and it tickled him to picture Mendel looking down at Sprintza, who maybe comes up to his chest, and shaking the moment she opens her mouth. It became a kind of inside joke for us, something we could always use to make the other one laugh. I know that this time it will not be that kind of visit.

The next day, thousands of people—Jews, old and young, sick and well, bearded, with *yarmulke*s, and clean shaven—wheel their carts onto our streets. They are sobbing and praying and it is a nightmare. All the pinching I do cannot wake me up.

Mendel and his family arrive. They come pushing a wheelbarrow loaded with their things, looking exhausted and sad and shocked. Their flat eyes stare into nothing.

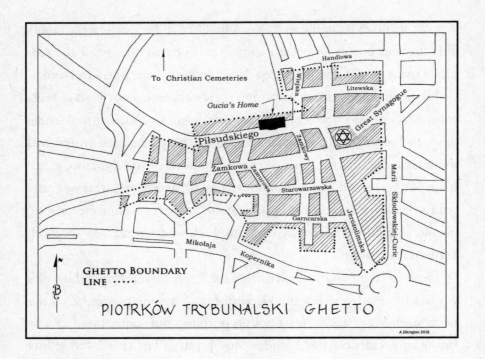

PIOTRKÓW TRYBUNALSKI GHETTO

GHETTO BOUNDARY LINE ·····

A. Elkington 2018

I see Heniek, and we hug but we are both in such shock we can no longer feel ourselves or each other. The sparkle has gone out of his eyes. More of his beautiful curly brown hair is falling out.

The next day Heniek comes with the first good news we've had since September 1. He has just heard that Baila Reichmann's construction supplies store is to be kept open. The Nazis need those materials and are keeping Leon and Baila in place to provide them. The Reichmanns have been designated essential workers and, for now, are safe.

The worst part of this new life is the utter helplessness—not knowing what is to come, knowing only that nothing we do matters. Yet my restless mind cannot stop churning, looking for a way out of this quicksand. With the good news of Pani Reichmann, I can clutch on to this thin thread of hope. Here is a problem I can put my mind to solving.

Maybe we can find a way to be essential, useful workers as well. It may be no more than a game I play in my mind, but it keeps me from going crazy or exploding in rage.

Suddenly I'm struck by the bitter irony. A few short years ago, when I was in torment over whether to quit Hashomer Hatsair, I decided that subjugating myself to some outside authority's dictates over my life's work—especially if I thought those dictates stupid or unjust—would be an intolerable punishment. Now to be an essential worker who is told what to do is my deepest wish.

The Germans come to our building again. They take all of Hela's trousseau, all her beautiful laces and linens. They empty all the jewelry from the jewelry box on her dresser, including the gold locket with the only photo of Jacob that she has. Mama's diamond ring is still safe in the hem of her coat and the candlesticks are at the bottom of the dirty laundry in a basket on the kitchen floor.

Mama and Tatte have never stayed home before. They've always worked so hard and had so many goals and challenges and successes. Now they walk from room to room of our apartment like ghosts. At least Mama can sew and clean and cook a little. There is Marek to play with and Regina to hug. The rebbitzin and Lulek come to visit. Lulek and Marek go off and play in the backyard. We cannot permit them to go to the street; it's too dangerous. But even in the backyard, they're terrified of the Nazis' dogs. We assure them that the animals can't get over the wall and that the backyard is safe, but they are both having nightmares about those vicious flesh-eating beasts. And my poor *tatte*, once so capable and easygoing and respected, is now like an empty shell. His armchair gone, he looks shrunken, sitting on a hard dining room chair, staring at the wall. And it has been barely two months since the Nazis started turning our world upside down.

Little by little, day by day, hour by hour, we feel the evil. It's as if we've been engulfed by a huge dark thundercloud and will never, ever see a blue sky or sunshine again. Each day there is a new proclamation posted on the buildings, a new order shouted at us from the streets with loudspeakers and bullhorns. Now I need to cover my ears and not understand the horrible sounds of a language I once loved. Each day a new demand. Jews must come and register all their gold. Jews must come and register all their furs. Jews must register all their diamonds and rubies and emeralds. Our possessions and properties and occupations, our lives reduced to inventories and lists. Each day, the Nazis chip away at us, and we become more and more numb as the days go by.

How much can we be ripped apart like this, day after day? It's not just our things we're being robbed of, but even our memories of who we are. We have become sad, floating creatures trying to make it through each nightmarish day. Eating, sleeping, trying to stay alive with no real sense of our past or our future. I do not recognize my home. It's like looking in the mirror and seeing a stranger. I am finding it harder and harder to remember what it felt like to be a happy, secure human being with rights and pride and a future. I wonder how long I can live this way without becoming the inferior creature they want me to be.

The Nazis have ratcheted up the violence. Until now, they have stolen our possessions and taken the occasional random life just for sport. But now they are using the lists the Community Council gave them to round up all the professionals, like teachers and lawyers. Some have tried to escape to Russia. But there is no warning, no time to plan. The Nazis come in the middle of the night and just drag people from their beds, in their pajamas with no shoes, no identification papers, and no time to kiss their wives or children or their *mezuzot* on the doorposts, leaving them no time to say a final goodbye.

Some are taken out and shot, and others just disappear. Not one of them has come back.

NOVEMBER 23, 1939

For us, the days go on and on in their monotony. There are too many people in our house and too little food. And now there is no salt. There is no coffee. There is no sugar. We have no more meat. There is nothing to do except clean and wash. Every day I stand in lines trying to buy stale, coarse dark bread and old potatoes tinged with green, with fat white eyes that look as if maggots are trying to crawl out. The few times I can find a cabbage or carrots I feel a brief flash of delight. Sometimes I am even able to find an onion.

And today the Nazis proclaim that all Jews must wear an armband. We are forced to buy white cloth to make the band and then, with blue thread, to embroider a Jewish star.

We must wear this band on our right arm whenever we are in public and if we do not have this by December 1, we will be killed. The monotony is now broken by our industrious sewing for everyone in our family.

The winter is very cold. We have to use the wood of our back fence to stoke the oven. Not having the protection of our fence allows some people to come in during the night and take down our precious wooden gazebo for firewood. Then they come and dismantle the stable. It's hard to feel anger at them. At least we have our own home, crowded as it is, and we have such a magnificent large yellow-tiled floor-to-ceiling oven in the kitchen that we can all stay relatively warm.

The constant fear and strain has made us all like zombies. Now Sprintza rarely speaks and Mendel is too hollow to care. Hela has not heard from Jacob for six months and there is a rumor that he was captured by the Russians and is in a Polish prisoner-of-war camp. Even Marek and Lulek play more quietly and sadly now. Without the fence protecting the backyard, they are too afraid of the vicious German dogs to go outside. The days go on and on, endlessly, and every moment we are hungry.

Labor Camps

ARBEIT MACHT FREI (Work sets you free)
—Sign on the entrance gate to the Auschwitz
Concentration Camp

1940

Early one morning in October we are startled awake by a loud knock on our door. It's Szymon Warszawski, deputy president of the *Judenrat*. He stands there with another man. He tells us that my brothers Josek and Idek are each to bring a small suitcase and report to the Nazi headquarters immediately. They are young and strong and are now to go to Lublin to help build a defense line for the Germans in case the Russians try to take over that part of Poland.

Our blood runs cold. Lublin is a six-hour train ride away. We panic that we may never see them again. Because I can speak German, Mama tells me to go to the headquarters. I must explain that we cannot be without the help of my brothers. And, if they must go to work, at least let them go somewhere close so that they can come home for the nights.

For the first time in over a year I put on a nice blue dress and comb my hair carefully. I put a little Coty powder on my face, a little lipstick on my lips, pinch my cheeks, put on that hated armband, and go to Nazi headquarters. After sitting in an outer office for thirty minutes, trying to pretend I am somewhere else, I am brought by a secretary to the SS man's office. I speak in my best German to the Nazi in charge. I say that my brothers cannot go to work. They are needed at home. The commander compliments me on my fine German and my elegant appearance, especially for a Jew. Then he smiles at me and politely says, "Either your brothers can come alive or they can come dead, but they will come."

It takes all my will to remain calm, because inside I am in a rage. I know there is nothing I can say or do. But at that moment in my heart I rebel. I swear to myself that I will never again submit to their will.

And so, that afternoon, with bitter tears, we hug and kiss Josek and Idek. We say a final farewell. We are all sure that this will be the last time we see our dear boys. They quietly take their small suitcases and they are gone.

Each day we hope for some word but nothing comes. And then after one week, a miracle: they return! They do not want to talk about their experiences, and truthfully, we do not want to hear.

A few days later, Rebbitzin Lau comes to us very disturbed. It has been exactly one year since the ghetto was formed and we have so many desperate people forced in from the outskirts of Piotrków and Kalisz and Łódź crowded in these small apartments. There is such need and, from the beginning, the rebbitzin has been helping to feed and take care of people at the orphanage and at the soup kitchen. This October day, she comes to tell us that a typhus epidemic has broken out in the ghetto. We have always feared that, of course: too many people living too close together, not enough fresh food, and not enough water or soap to keep ourselves or our clothes clean. Those lice can live anywhere.

They are so tiny and so hard to see. Once they bite you, you get that wretched disease in your blood, and once it is in the home, everyone is in danger.

The *Judenrat* sets up a sanitary service to keep apartments clean and to empty the containers from the people who have no toilets. Josek, Idek, and even Beniek volunteer to do that horrible work. Our relatives from Kalisz and Łódź, especially Hinda, are busy washing, washing, washing all our clothes and we carefully inspect each other's seams and hair for lice whenever we come in from the streets.

The typhus epidemic is all we talk about now. Rumors are that over one thousand people have died from it, thousands more have been horribly sick. Every day we see mourners following pine coffins, and little children walking in the streets with shaved heads, to keep the lice from crawling on them. So far none of us in our apartment building has been touched by the typhus. We just boil and wash and check the seams and bathe and boil and wash and check the seams and bathe again.

Heniek

Love goes toward love, as schoolboys from their books;
But love from love, toward school with heavy looks.
—William Shakespeare, *Romeo and Juliet*

MAY 1941

The ghetto is so gray and colorless that it feels impossible spring will ever come. Idek has just given me a letter from Heniek.

He begins by proclaiming his deep love for me and his wish not to cause me any worry, but says that he and Josek left by train last night to smuggle themselves into Russia. Heniek writes that we all know life will only get worse here in the ghetto. Rumors of deportations and concentration camps and extermination are everywhere, and he and Josek feel they must see if there is a possibility for all of us to escape to a better life in Russia. I show the letter to Mama and she cries. I feel sick and frightened. We are so worried and pray they will be safe.

We hear nothing for three weeks and then, a knock on the door and there they are! Triumphant! What a difference from when Josek was at the door returning from the labor camp in Lublin. This Josek is smiling and laughing and talking about their adventures.

Heniek hugs me and asks me to go for a walk. As I clutch his warm hand, he tells me that it was easy for them to get across the border from Poland to Russia. They just got off the train at the stop before the new Soviet border and walked across to the little town of Kovel. There were no soldiers there at all. Heniek believes that if we go to Russia and then move farther east, far from the border, we will be safe from the Germans and the war. He begs me to go with him. I am in shock. I tell him that I need to think about it, and he seems bewildered.

"Gucia, what possible good can come from staying here? We have loved each other for ten years and shared so many dreams for the future. What do you need to think about?"

But going to Russia with Heniek means getting married, and I just don't feel ready to make this commitment. Of course I love Heniek, just as I love my family. But shouldn't being in love feel absolutely certain, almost like there's no choice? Is what we feel for each other really true love? And I don't know. I want to be sure. Am I numb and empty because of the war or is there a part of me numb and empty because I don't really love Heniek?

For a painful week we argue and discuss this major decision.

I finally have to say, "No!"

I cannot tell him the truth. I cannot say, "No, I am not ready to marry you. I am not sure I love you." I lie and say I am too afraid to take the risk, and that I cannot leave my family at a time like this. I urge Heniek to go, to save himself.

But he says he could never go without me. We hug each other and part. After that conversation, it's no longer the same between us. Slowly, we stop seeing each other. And this time, he doesn't write to me and try to win me back.

Hendla Libeskind Gomolinska

Love thy wife as thyself; honor her more than thyself.
He who lives unmarried, lives without joy.
If thy wife is small, bend down to her
and whisper in her ear.
He who sees his wife die, has, as it were, been present
At the destruction of the sanctuary itself.
—Rabbi Shimon ben Lakish,
also known as Reish Lakish (c. 200 CE–c. 275 CE)

JULY–OCTOBER 1941

Mama is stirring the potato soup and asks me to get her an aspirin. She has a headache. It is so hot and humid, and stirring the soup makes her hotter. Her face is bright red and I am a little concerned. She brushes me away.

"No! No, I'm fine. Nothing is wrong. It's just too hot."

I go to the bathroom to find the aspirin, and when I get back she is lying on the kitchen floor, the dripping soup spoon in her hand. I scream. Hela and Regina and Sprintza and Mendel and Tatte and Beniek all come running, and we carry her to her bed.

She is burning hot. I bathe Mama with alcohol and put cool compresses on her face. I open her blouse to put cool cloths on her breast and I see the ugly truth. There it is. There is an angry red rash on her chest. Little red dots running all over those breasts that once fed and comforted her eight children. No! It's not possible! For nine months we have checked all of our clothes and hair and seams. Not one louse has been found in our apartment. We have boiled and cleaned and boiled and cleaned for nine months. Mama cannot be sick.

We fear spreading the typhus. Like the homes of every family stricken with this disease, our apartment is quarantined. For the next two weeks I alone care for her all day and sleep with her each night. Everyone else must avoid contact with her. I know this puts me in greater danger of catching it, too, but I try not to think about it.

Mama is getting worse, so with most of the little money we have left, we hire a nurse from the hospital to come every day. Sister is very gentle and kind. She bathes Mama and tries to make her comfortable. Mama is so weak. She has no strength to talk, to hold up her head, to smile. The rabbi says that the name of this disease comes from the Greek word *typhos*, meaning smoky, and that is how Mama's brain and body must feel. Wispy and weak and foggy and smoky.

When Sister leaves in the evenings, I get into bed with Mama and I murmur soothing words to her before falling asleep myself. Then one night I say, "Mama, I'm going to sing to you." There is a little smile on her face. I realize that even through the smoke and fog of her fever, she must be remembering my teenage humiliation at Hashomer Hatsair. We were singing and dancing and I was having such a great time, when Heniek said to me, "Gucia, you really have a terrible voice!" I was so mortified and hurt that I never sang again from that time on. But now I will try anything that might bring her comfort. I sing "Gadolfs Rein," the song she always sang to us as children.

I don't need fancy dresses
I don't need money
I need only my beautiful children
To conquer the world.

I sing this lullaby over and over, thinking what Mama sang is true. As long as we have each other our world still belongs to us. And she puts her hot, hot hand on my head.

The next day, Sister tells me she is going to go to Ogrod Bernardinski, the park on Slowackiego Street outside the ghetto.

"Praise God that it is July," she says. "The lindens are blooming and they are the sacred tree of the Blessed Mother."

She goes to gather blossoms to make linden tea. It will make Mama sweat and break her fever. I envy Sister for being free to walk wherever she wants without applying for special permission or having to wear an armband. The idea of just strolling to the park any moment you feel like it—that life is over. But even just imagining the lindens, so magnificent this time of year, and their sweet smell, soothes and calms me a bit. I pray to the God of Abraham, Isaac, and Jacob (hoping Mother Mary might overhear) that the tea will work.

When Sister returns, she boils the water and throws in the blossoms and I find a little bit of honey still left in the old beehive of the apple tree. But Mama cannot swallow anything. We try many times, spooning little drops of the healing tea into her mouth, but it just dribbles back out.

"Maybe tomorrow," says Sister, and leaves for the day.

I climb into bed with Mama and sing to her. It's now been three weeks since Mama fainted on the kitchen floor, the potato soup ladle in her hand, and even though I keep putting cool cloths on her, she is still so hot. She thrashes around and her eyes are glassy. But the rash is gone.

It is sweltering hot outside. Maybe it's not the fever at all, but just the summer heat and humidity. I feel hot, too, and exhausted, and a little sick, weak, shaky.

By midnight Mama seems to settle down. She swallows a drop of the linden tea. I go out and share this tiny glimmer of hope with the rest of the family. Until now the risk of contagion has kept everyone out of the room, but Tatte can't stand it anymore. He sticks his head in the bedroom doorway to talk to her, and I leave them alone for a while. When Tatte leaves, I crawl back into bed with Mama. I wish I could hold her burning, trembling, bone-thin body close to mine, the way she would hold me and all the children when we were little. But she is so hot and her skin so sensitive, holding her would not be comforting but only add to her suffering.

"Mamashi," I chant, "please get well. We need you."

I am beyond tired but somehow I drift off to sleep.

I wake with a start. It's already dawn. I see a little bit of sunlight and hear some birds singing. And Mama is so much better. Her fever has broken during the night. She is cool. The tea must have worked. I am so relieved and happy. I hug her and then I realize: She is not cool. She is cold. Ice cold. I scream, "Mama! Mama! Mama!"

Everyone in the house comes running. But it's over. My mama, the person most dear to me in all the world, is dead.

I feel like I have died along with my mama. I feel totally numb and distant. My body still functions, but it's as if there's no one inside. I give Mama one last bath. I feel like a machine making jerky little actions. I am so dried up I have no tears. I dress my mama in a lovely white gown.

Tante Sura comes and covers the mirrors with white cloths just like when my baby sister, Rifka, died. My uncles and cousins come to join Tatte for the ten-man *minyan* to recite the mourners' prayer for Mama.

And we need to praise God that Josek and Idek can be with us. They have been trying to volunteer for work at the glass factories of Kara and Hortensja and the woodworking camp in Bugaj, where strong young men can gain safety as essential workers. If they'd been chosen, we would have been sitting *shiva* missing the two oldest sons to say Kaddish for our dead mama.

Tatte makes the sounds of prayer but there is no force or spirit in his words. It seems there is no one left inside either of us. We are just empty. Only a few people come to visit. Mama was so loved, but everyone is afraid of catching typhus. As we get ready for the funeral, the rabbi tears the left side of my dress to show my mourning. It's all such a blur.

Four Jewish policemen knock on our door. They have come to escort us because the Jewish cemetery is three kilometers outside the ghetto, and we need special permission to bury our own Jewish mother in her own Jewish grave. We place Mama's plain pine coffin in the ground next to her two baby daughters, our redheaded sisters, Rifka and Chanusck.

I go through the motions of comforting a sobbing Regina. I envy her. She is able to cry. But I feel dead inside and Tatte seems the same. There have been so many deaths; this is just another one for the ghetto. But for our family it is like the end of the world.

The weeks pass into months and I feel as if the Gucia I used to be has died with Mama. I care nothing for life and feel nothing except hunger. The only actions I take are the duties of caring for the family, and the housekeeping that Mama used to do.

I go out every day to find rotten potatoes and wilted cabbage and wrinkled carrots. It hardly matters. We are starving and eat whatever we can find, even though we almost choke on the moldy potatoes.

My poor family. Now they have to depend on me to feed them. The only thing I know how to make is potato soup. And that's what we eat, or at least what I call what we eat, day after day. In October, Josek and Idek go to work at the labor camp at Bugaj.

I didn't think the house could feel more empty, but it does. I do nothing. I just wait for what comes next, not caring, not caring about anything at all.

The Beginning of the End

One way or another—I will tell you quite openly—
we must finish off the Jews.
—Hans Frank (1900–1946), governor of occupied Poland,
December 16, 1941

MAY–AUGUST 1942

They sealed the Piotrków ghetto tight last month. What did it matter to us? What more could they do? Before, we could put on those hated blue-and-white armbands and go out before the curfew. Now we are animals trapped in our cage.

We kept hearing more and more horror stories about Jews being taken off to be systematically killed—not just men but women and children, old people. We heard that the Jews were put in trucks or trains or marched, shot in forests, or put in work camps and concentration camps where thousands died from illness and exhaustion. True, we had seen the cruelty of the Nazis from that very first day in September 1939: the blood flowing in our streets, the humiliation, the beards cruelly torn off the faces of the old Hasids, the vicious dogs terrifying the children, but that was just a few madmen. Some soldiers are always brutal. We couldn't believe that the whole country of Germany—a culture that gave the world Mozart and Beethoven and Brahms, Goethe and Heine and Schiller, a culture of brilliance and elegance—could methodically be planning the final extermination of the Jews. It just could not be true. It had to be hysterical rumors of war.

Many years before the war, Heniek and I had read parts of Hitler's *Mein Kampf.* It was frightening and disturbing, but mostly we thought it was rambling and boring. We had wanted to understand who this chancellor of Germany was. He published his book in 1925, raging about "the Jewish peril." We understood that Hitler viewed the Germans, the Aryans, as *Übermenschen*, supermen, and we Jews were as low as the Germans were high. Hitler said that Jews were parasites and maggots and bloodsuckers and monsters and filthy and that we Jews were conspiring to keep the Aryans from ruling the world. At the end of *Mein Kampf* Hitler suggested that twelve to fifteen thousand Jews should have been gassed during World War I instead of the German soldiers.

We saw what horrors Hitler created in Germany in the 1930s, especially the horror of Kristallnacht. And yet, with all the venom and anti-Semitism and racism and hatred and murder and destruction, we had heard it all before. The possibility that Hitler planned to exterminate all the Jews never entered our minds. We had survived pogroms before and we could survive them again.

By December 1941 America had finally entered the war and we knew that, in the end, America would win. We simply needed to hold on, be patient, and wait it out.

Now Uncle Josef comes to live with us. He is afraid the authorities will come after him at his home because of the rumors that his son, Janek, has escaped the ghetto. This is true. He tells us that Janek has been living as a gentile in Warsaw, where he has Polish connections and some money. Instead of Janek Libeskind, he is now Yannick Zarzycki. He is trying to get false identity papers for his sister Mala and his mother, Sura. They both have blond hair and blue eyes and speak perfect Polish. Uncle Josef, with his brown eyes, dark, curly hair, and Yiddish accent, knows that he can never pass.

We'd heard rumors of some Jews living as Poles outside the ghetto, yet I couldn't believe this was really possible. The rebbitzin has been urging me to leave for months. With my fair hair and coloring and my perfect Polish and German, she thinks I have a chance. And I have no husband or children to worry about. Now that the ghetto is sealed, time is of the essence. We have news of the German *Aktions*—mass deportations of the Jews and liquidation of their ghettos in towns near us. The rebbitzin thinks the rumors of the exterminations are true, and each day they are getting closer to Piotrków. She urges me to get out of the ghetto as soon as I can.

Jews have been gassed at Chelmno. There are prison camps in Bełżec and Malkinia. Lublin and Radom are all *Judenrein*.

For the past year, since Mama died, I've been frozen in depression. To think and decide and take any kind of action is impossible. But we know from the movement of the Nazis that liquidation of the Piotrków ghetto is just weeks away. Somehow the urgency of this danger shakes me back to life. I will face a terrible risk of getting caught, and I know that those who get caught get killed. But what about the risk of staying?

My depression lifts. Now I feel rage, the same feeling that made me swear to myself, when pleading with the Nazi colonel to spare Idek and Josek, that I will never submit to them. And there's something else, a kind of recklessness. After all that's happened since that meeting, in a way life feels cheap, almost like there's less to lose; and if I fail, at least it's my choice how it ends.

Now that I've decided I act quickly. I've heard rumors that you can buy false identification papers at a house on Zamkowa Street.

Fortunately I still have a spare photo from the ones I'd had taken for my university identification card. I grab some money from my minuscule savings and hurry to the address. It is amazing: there in broad daylight a Jewish man I have never seen before sits in the alcove of the doorway at a rickety table crowded with paper and pens and bottles of ink, rubber stamps and pads, and a typewriter. He is busily making entries in a large account book—I guess so that it looks like he's doing something legal.

I whisper what I want, he calmly tells me the price, and after I assure him I have the money, he asks me what name I want on my new *Kennkarte*. Oddly, I hadn't thought about that before I came.

Gomolinska could be a Polish name, but too many people know my family and our butcher shops. Sura Gitla is a dead giveaway that I am a Jew. Last names come flying into my head. Lewinova, after my old home economics teacher? Grabowska, the teacher I carried the books for? Tretiak, after the horrible professor who failed the Jewish boy in Warsaw?

And my first name, should I be a Krysia or a Magda or an Ana? I don't know why, but suddenly Danuta pops up, the name of the little daughter of the peasants in Przyglow. So perfectly Polish. And the name Barbara. It's a name common to both Germans and Poles and sometimes even Jews. I'd always loved that name, which was very popular when I was a small child. And how very apt. It means barbarian. It means alien, it means stranger. Yes!

And then for a last name, Tanska. It just comes—from where, I don't know. But it is pure Polish. Perfect.

He is waiting with a pen in hand and a piece of scrap paper, and I know I need to get this over with.

"Danuta Barbara Tanska," I say confidently, not a quiver in my voice. I spell it for him as he writes it down. We work out other details, too: date of birth, address, and so forth.

Then he gets to work. From between two pages at the back of his account book, he removes what I assume is a phony blank *Kennkarte*. Relieved, I see he's using a gray-colored lightweight cardboard paper. That's what the Poles have for their identification; not the yellow cardboard that's used for the Jews. He rolls the card into the typewriter and taps out all the information I gave him, starting with *Danuta Barbara Tanska*. These names could mean my survival. Then he removes the form from the machine. I hand him my photo and he glues it onto the gray paper. Next, after punching holes in two corners of the photo, he taps two tiny metal grommets in place to further secure it. He shows me where to sign the card and, using a black stamp pad, I add in two fingerprints. After that, he takes a blue-inked rubber stamp and presses it down onto the corner of the photo and a bit of the paper. Then he folds the cardboard in two places, making it a three-page booklet. The papers look good enough for casual inspection, though if anyone were suspicious and scrutinized them carefully, I could be in trouble. My hand shakes as I pay him his five hundred *zlotys*; he gives me the paper and I scurry home. I breathe deeply and feel a sense of hope. Danuta Barbara Tanska will try to survive this horror and be a witness to it.

When I return home, I show my father my new *Kennkarte* and tell him I have decided to hide from the Germans. We've all heard of Poles in the Christian part of Piotrków who are willing to hide a Jew in their homes in exchange for money. My plan is to live outside the ghetto for a month or so while the Nazis carry out the deportations of Jews from Piotrków, and then when things have had a chance to settle down and the Germans have moved on to the next town, I will return to the ghetto.

My *tatte* is furious. He stands up and shouts, "No! I will not permit this! Whatever happens to us we face together. You will not separate from the family!"

I argue back with my father. "Tatte, I know it would be too dangerous for anyone but me to try this. You and the boys look Jewish, and the Nazis immediately check any men they suspect, for their mark of circumcision. Regina is too young, and Hela has Marek. Even Chaya Lau says my looks could pass, and I have no other attachments. Isn't it better that at least one of us takes the chance to remain free?"

And for the first time in my life, my father slaps me hard across the face. My father, who has never lifted his hand to anyone in his life. Then he crumples in the chair and sobs.

Uncle Josef speaks in my defense. "Itzak, you cannot take the responsibility for Gucia's life in your hands. She has the right to decide her own fate. It is her life." Uncle Josef says this quietly, and my father nods his consent.

That slap. I will never forget the shock and the secret glow. My *tatte* really does love me. Now I don't just know it; I feel it.

Over the next few days I work out the details and now I am ready to go. Hela's brother-in-law, Jacob's brother Abek, knows a Polish woman who buys clothes from their factory. She sells these to some of the less well-off Poles who can't afford the custom-made garments of a tailor or seamstress. We have seen her when she has come to the ghetto to do business with Abek. She is not particularly refined or principled, but for a large payment she is willing to take me into her home. I pack a small suitcase. In it I put my favorite dress, peach colored with leather trimmings, and a few others, including two that were Mama's. I add some underwear and toiletries. I take no photos. The only jewelry is the watch Mama gave me as a reward for the high praise from my ninth-grade teacher, and the ruby ring she gave me when I was accepted to the university in Jerusalem. I have a little money and put it in my bra and carry some change and my new Polish identification card in my purse.

By now it is August and a month after the first *yahrtzeit*, the anniversary of my mama's death. I hug Regina and Hela and Marek and Mendel and Sprintza and Beniek and Uncle Josef, and I hold my sobbing *tatte* very close.

"Please give my love to Josek and Idek," I whisper into Tatte's ear. I pray that their work at the labor camp will protect them from deportation, and I wonder if I will ever see any of my family again. I put my armband in a drawer and leave.

I go across the hall to the Laus' to say goodbye and I give the rebbitzin a little note for Heniek. Even if I am no longer in love with him, I will always love him. He was my first love. God forbid he should be the last. Then I hurry downstairs, go out the front door, and I am on my own. It is well past curfew and I walk into the dark, avoiding the main streets by going through a maze, over garden walls and through the inner courtyards of buildings to the back of the ghetto. I push my small suitcase through a crack in the ghetto wall, squeeze my thin body after it, and I am out. With my suitcase in my sweating hand, I walk through the dark Christian cemetery to the address that Abek has given me.

It is a small house. I knock and the unsmiling Polish woman quickly opens the door. She takes my suitcase and shows me to my room on the ground floor and disappears. The room faces the street and there are no curtains on the windows. Anyone walking past can look right in. This is no place to hide. I am horrified to realize that I have been tricked. It is too dangerous to stay here. I can't turn on a light. In the daytime, people will see me in a room with only a little furniture and no curtains and they will know that I do not belong. I knock loudly on the woman's door and demand that she give me back my suitcase, but she doesn't answer. I keep knocking. Again and again. Louder and louder. Nothing. My knees are shaking and I feel sick. In despair, I walk back through the dark streets of Polish Piotrków, creeping silently through the Christian cemetery and back into the ghetto. I am home, and I have failed.

Some days pass as I try to think of what to do next. Hela is sitting on her balcony one day, looking out onto Piłsudskiego Street, and she sees the Polish woman who stole my suitcase. Hela starts screaming to the Jewish police on the street, "Get her! Get her! She is a thief. Just ask Abek."

Everyone knows Abek. He's an excellent tailor and runs the family's uniform-making business, so he has wonderful connections with both the Jewish police and the Nazis. The policemen grab the woman and take her to Abek. He makes her promise to return my things to me this very day; he warns her that if she does not, she will face prison. Imagine! Jewish police are protecting me from being exploited by a Pole. I feel ashamed to remember how I had despised anyone who would join the Jewish police for betraying their own people to serve the Germans. Again I see that what's right and moral is not always black and white.

She does bring back my suitcase, but she keeps my favorite peach dress with the leather trimmings. I am learning more than at university. I now understand that the only person you can trust with certainty is yourself.

Escape from the Ghetto

Submit to me as soon as possible a draft showing . . .
the measures already taken for the execution of the
intended final solution of the Jewish question.
—Reichsmarschall Hermann Göring (1893–1946),
in a directive dated July 31, 1941

SEPTEMBER 1942

The Nazis are getting more and more brutal with each passing day. From the radio we follow their course as the army "progresses" from city to city, deporting Jews. They are proud to announce it! The Germans are so methodical and relentless. That our turn is about to come, that our ghetto is about to be liquidated is as inevitable as geography. What will happen after that is the subject of wild rumors: atrocities even worse than anything we've imagined before.

The rebbitzin comes to talk to me privately. We go out to the garden. The gazebo is long gone, having been broken apart for firewood, but my old gnarled apple tree is still there and we sit in the shade.

"I know those horrible stories are true. Gucia, you have to try to save yourself. The German soldiers will be here in less than a week to begin the deportations. You cannot wait even one day longer. Don't be afraid. Your Polish is perfect and you don't look or sound like a Jew. Your forged papers are good enough. Go, be Danuta Barbara Tanska, and get out of Piotrków. Get out, now."

She thinks the safest thing for me to do is to go to the resort town of Nowy Sącz.

"We have heard that it is now completely *Judenrein*," she says. She takes my hand. "No one would suspect that a Jew would go there as a tourist."

"*Judenrein?* Nowy Sącz? How can that be?" I ask.

Nowy Sącz had more Jews than Piotrków! Maybe twenty-five thousand. Itka Moskowitz and I had always wanted to go there when we were in Kraków, but we never found the time. I remember hearing that it was a famous and cultured place for the Hasidim, with a beautiful synagogue from the eighteenth century. How could there be no Jews?

"They emptied the ghetto within three days. They sent over twenty thousand Jews to a camp called Bełżec. Gucia, go tonight," she whispers urgently.

In my desperation, I put all my hopes into the only solution I can come up with, to go for help to Pan Dobranski, the kind and honest Pole who used to live behind our property. I often tutored his son, and I feel deep affection for the family. We were all so sad when the Nazis forced them to move away. God forbid that a Pole should live near a Jew after the ghetto was formed.

He had left his address and I know that he has moved to the area called the Schweinemarkt. Pan Dobranski looks like a typical Pole, tall, sturdy, blond, with clear blue eyes and a friendly, open face. If he travels with me on the train I will be less likely to be suspected.

His first name, Kazimierz, is the same as that of the enlightened king who welcomed Jewish immigration into Poland in 1334. Maybe this is a sign, and the namesake of that great king will give me sanctuary.

I pack a small suitcase. I say goodbye to my family. I do not cry. Tatte tries to give me Mama's diamond ring, but I refuse. If they are deported he must keep it. He might need that money to feed and take care of our family.

Again I take off my hated armband and sneak out of the ghetto late at night after curfew, with my small suitcase in my sweating hand. Again I squeeze through a crack in the ghetto wall, and walk in the pitch-dark through the Christian cemetery.

I'm barely breathing.

I go to the address I had memorized, careful to stay away from busy streets. If Pan Dobranski turns me away I don't know what I will do. I knock. I wait.

What will happen if he's not there? I can't possibly go back to the ghetto.

I feel so exposed. But he does open the door and I realize I have been holding my breath since I knocked. He greets me with shock, but then he smiles warmly and hurries me inside his house. Helping a Jew escape the ghetto puts him in great danger, of course, but he doesn't hesitate a moment.

I am so relieved by his reaction that I must force myself to hold back tears. I ask if he will let me spend the night in his house and then go to Nowy Sącz with me on the first train in the morning.

I offer to pay him for the great risk he will be taking. He tells me that his family has often worried about us and hoped that we were safe. He says he is happy to return the help to me as I was so helpful to his son, and of course he will go with me to Nowy Sącz. He says there is a daily train that leaves at seven in the morning.

We drink some hot tea and then he shows me a little cot behind a curtain in the kitchen. I am exhausted and fall asleep immediately.

In the middle of the night I wake up with a start. Someone is getting onto the cot; someone large who smells very bad, of sweat and vodka and filth.

He whispers, "I am the brother-in-law of Kazimierz! You are so beautiful."

I am more enraged than frightened. Even though he could denounce me as a Jew, I angrily whisper that if he doesn't leave me alone, immediately, I will scream so loudly the roof will fall in.

He seems surprised, disappointed. How could I refuse this great gift he is offering? What nerve! He leaves and I spend the rest of the night sitting up in the bed shaking with fear and anger and disgust.

Hugging my knees, shivering on my small cot, I realize that it has been only five hours since I was saying goodbye to my family in the ghetto.

In the early morning, Pan Dobranski and I walk to the train station. I give him the money we had agreed upon. As we walk through the train station I see an old *babushka* sitting alone on a bench. It's my aunt Sura! Our eyes meet and then we quickly look away. I pray that we both make it out of this nightmare. My heart is pounding as I search for police in the crowd; if I am discovered, Pan Dobranski will be denounced. Pangs of guilt rush through me.

Fortunately, it is unseasonably cold and we are covered up; no one will notice who we are or wonder why we do not talk to each other. We board the train.

I am hoping Pan Dobranski hadn't noticed my panic after the train first left the station, when I couldn't find my *Kennkarte* and started desperately hunting through my pockets for it. I didn't want to make him afraid that I might give us away.

It is at least two hours after we have settled into our seats before I feel the tension start to drain from my aching muscles. For the rest of our six-hour journey I feel blessedly still. At least for now I have nothing to do but be invisible.

I wish the train would never stop and I could stay in this empty state forever—be nowhere and feel nothing and be no one. But I know that soon enough we will arrive and I will have to begin the work of transforming into someone else: a simple Polish girl named Basia.

The truth is, I've always had such a terror of public humiliation, ever since those embarrassing early weeks of first grade. So from a young age I cultivated a manner that would not draw attention to myself. People have often said that before they got to know me, they thought I was reserved or shy. Now there is a lot more at stake than humiliation, and I am counting on this natural camouflage to help save my life.

As we get close to Nowy Sącz my heart starts to race. We pull into the station and it is like coming out of a dreamless sleep into a waking nightmare.

Pan Dobranski gets off the train with me, walks to the street, hugs me, and then disappears back into the train station to return to Piotrków.

I pick up my suitcase and walk to the center of town.

Nowy Sącz

Suspense is worse than the ordeal.
—Yiddish proverb

SEPTEMBER 1942

Walking to the center of this charming little town in southern Poland, I find a crowded café, buy a newspaper, and sip my tea while reading the advertisements for rooms for rent. I go to seven different apartments and they all say the vacancy has been filled.

Are they afraid to rent to me because they suspect I'm a Jew?

It's getting very late and starting to rain, so I go to a guesthouse and take a room for the week. They demand that I leave my ID because the police come every evening to check who is staying there. I sleep very little that night.

For the next few days I wander around beautiful, peaceful Nowy Sącz. There is an enormous, picturesque old marketplace similar to the Rynek of Kraków. Past the city hall I see the old castle of Kazimierz the Great and the now-empty ghetto.

I quickly avert my eyes from that painful vacancy and determine never to go near that sad area again.

The lovely River Dunajec has made Nowy Sącz famous for its therapeutic baths and spas. The rebbitzin was right. This is a perfect place for a Polish transient like me. Maybe the waters are truly therapeutic. I begin to relax, breathe deeply, and feel the tight band across my chest loosen a little.

Every morning I wake up when the sun shines through the window, dress, and go to a café and drink coffee. I buy the paper, read it in the park, stroll on the banks of the river, eat an apple for lunch, walk around the river again, go to a cheap restaurant and have soup for dinner, and walk around some more. There is no plan, no structure, except to avoid notice for one month until I can return to Piotrków. I am absolutely rudderless. The days feel endless.

My ID is working. The police have checked it each day and there are no questions so far. The owner of the guesthouse is friendly enough. The days melt into one another and my loneliness and worry about my family are almost unbearable.

Then one evening, as I am just about ready for bed, I hear a muffled knocking on my door. My heart stops and then pounds violently. When I open the door I see two men standing there whom I recognize from the Piotrków ghetto. They say they are staying in the room just next door: two brothers, their wives, and a mother-in-law.

At first they were afraid to talk to me; there is no way to know who else might be under suspicion. But after a few days they figured it was safe. I am thrilled with this incredibly lucky coincidence. They invite me next door and I spend a nice evening visiting with them and their family. They have been in Nowy Sącz a few weeks already and the men have gotten jobs at Stowaszyszenie Odszcurzania Malapolski, the Southern Poland Extermination Company.

They mention that the company needs more workers and wants to hire women. One of the wives will be starting tomorrow. Am I

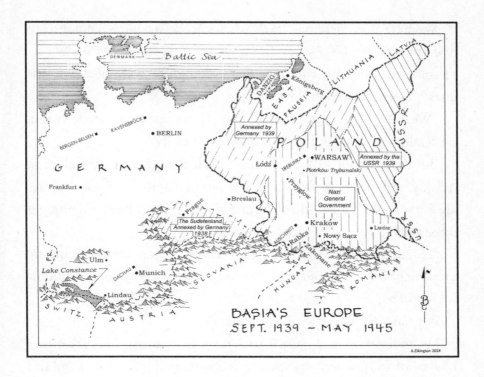

Annexed by
Germany 1939

Annexed by the
USSR 1939

Nazi
General
Government

The Sudetenland
Annexed by Germany
1938

BASIA'S EUROPE
SEPT. 1939 — MAY 1945

A.Elkington 2018

interested? I do need the money and working will help quiet my brain. But I cannot believe the irony! I have fled the extermination of the Nazis to find work in an extermination company!

In the morning the four of us go to work. We are to make sample packages of rat poison. Simple enough. A *Volksdeutsche*, a German who lives in Poland, works with us and shows us what to do. We take the little dried biscuits from the conveyor belt and put eighteen of them into a tin that has a picture of a dead rat lying on its back with its legs in the air, a skull and crossbones over it. The woman assures us that the biscuits are dangerous only to rats. They are made of flour and sugar and a toxic plant called red squill, but we are careful to wear gloves and as soon as we get home, we scrub our hands until they are raw.

We have been here one week when the *Volksdeutsche* comes to us and says that the Nazi supervisor has some concerns about us. We are to come back to meet with him that evening. We walk silently to the guesthouse and meet in their room.

"We must escape immediately," I say. "They suspect we are Jews and, especially for the men, they can find out so easily."

But they are not willing to flee. The older woman cannot move so quickly, and they have all their possessions in that room. Their suitcases are bursting with silver and china and clothing. They had even brought some small pieces of furniture.

"No, don't panic," they say. "This will be just another bureaucratic meeting of no consequence. If you run and they catch you, you know what will happen."

But I am certain we are in great danger.

I go to my room and quickly pack my small suitcase. I tell the owner I have just learned that my mother and sister will be in Zakopane and I am rushing to meet them. I pretend to be happy and excited that I will see them. I pay her for that night and she gives Danuta Barbara Tanska back her identification card.

By the time I set off for the train station the sun has set and it's starting to rain. The meeting with the Nazi supervisor is supposed to begin just moments from now.

I take the back roads to the train station, running in the dark on the slippery, uneven ground. There is no moon and I cannot see a thing. I keep falling and running, falling and running.

I keep looking back to see if I'm being chased. I pray to God that when I get to the train station I won't find the SS there waiting for me. The whole time my heart pounds so violently I'm afraid this might be what kills me. I have never been so frightened in my entire life.

As I sit on the station bench waiting, I expect the Nazis to come for me at any moment. I am a helpless observer, with my life at stake, watching to see who will win the race between the Nazis and the train.

For the fifteen minutes that I sit waiting, I concentrate all my energy on keeping still, freezing my face and watching the entrance, willing the train to come before the SS. At last a train pulls in, and I force myself to walk calmly and slowly onto the first car.

Once the train is under way and I settle down, my mind wanders, oddly enough, to my high school Hebrew teacher, Pan Rosenblum. He would ask us questions so fast and we had to give him an immediate answer without thinking. I resented him then, but now I feel deep gratitude. His training has helped me make a split-second decision. Without thinking, Basia is out of Nowy Sącz and on a train to another tourist resort. I am on my way to Rabka.

The train ride is not long. It's about ten p.m. when I disembark and go out into the pouring rain.

I realize I can't just show up at a guesthouse late at night sopping wet without arousing suspicion. So I find cover under a doorway where I spend the night standing and hoping the rain will end and I will have time to dry off before daylight, when people come into the street and might expose me.

Am I shaking from the fear or from the cold or from both? After a while the rain does stop. I walk to a park at dawn and try to get dry. I comb my hair and put on some lipstick. I must be a middle-class Polish tourist who is in Rabka for a little rest.

The guesthouse I find is very nice and I start to feel better. The sun is out and the sky is blue. But I am still chilled by the experience at the extermination company.

The next day I go to a pharmacy and buy some peroxide. I have always had ash-blond hair but I feel so frightened about being found out as a Jew, I go to my room and bleach my hair blonder. I bleach it so much that a lot of it breaks and falls off into the sink. Fortunately, it turns quite cold again and I can cover my hair with a kerchief.

Again, like in Nowy Sącz, there is nothing to do. I walk to a café and have coffee. I buy a newspaper and sit in the park. I eat an apple for lunch and walk around this beautiful little town at the foot of the Tatra Mountains. I walk some more and then I go to a café and have soup for dinner. How much longer will my money hold out? I go back to the guesthouse and try to sleep. Try to shut up my noisy brain.

What is happening in Piotrków?

CLAIMING MY PLACE
Photo Album

Piotrków Trybunalski street scenes, c. 1915 (above) and undated

Gucia's family home, 21 Piłsudskiego Street, Piotrków Trybunalski

The family of Leon Reichmann, Piotrków Trybunalski, Poland, 1920; Leon is second from left. No portrait of Gucia's family survived the war.

Gucia Gomolinska and Heniek Wajshof with their Hashomer Hatsair group, 1933

Heniek Wajshof, 1937

Rabbi Moshe Chaim Lau and Rebbitzin Chaya Lau

Gucia's childhood friends Rozia Nissenson, 1932, (left) and Sala Grinzspan, 1936

Gucia's brother Josek, c. 1938

German tanks and troops approach a village during the invasion of Poland,
September 1939

German police and soldiers in Piotrków Trybunalski, 1939

Two German police beside Piotrków Trybunalski ghetto sign, c. 1939

Sign in the Piotrków Trybunalski ghetto: "Jews are
not allowed to walk on this pavement"

BEKANNTMACHUNG | OBWIESZCZENIE.

Die Verwaltung der Jüdischen Gemeinde in Perikau bringt zur Kenntnis, dass zufolge Verordnung des Herrn Generalgouverneurs vom 24. Januar 1940 Juden im Generalgouvernement (Anordnung für den Kreis Petrikau Nr. 3/40)

zur Anmeldung ihres Vermögens bis zum 10. März 1940 verpflichtet sind.

Die hierzu erforderlichen amtlichen Formulare, die jede jüdische Person, die das 21 Lebensjahr beendete, auszufüllen hat, sind täglich in der Zeit vom 9 bis 13 und von 15 bis 17 Uhr im Gemeindelokal TÖPFER-GASSE 7 bis zum 8 März 1940 erhältlich.

Die ordnungsmässig ausgefüllten Formulare sind im obigen Lokal bis spätestens den 10. März 1940 abzugeben.

Die Verwaltung der Jüdischen Gemeinde weist darauf hin, dass jegliche Übertretung der obigen Verordnung mit Geld- und Gefängnisstrafen droht. Das nicht angemeldete Vermögen wird ausserdem als herrenlos betrachtet und UNTERLIEGT DER BESCHLAGNAHME.

DER PRÄSES des ÄLTESTENRATES der Jüdischen Gemeinde Petrikau

Zarząd Gminy Żydowskiej w Piotrkowie zawiadamia, że w myśl Rozp. Gen. Gub. z dn. 24 stycznia 1940 r.

o obowiązku zgłoszenia majątku

w Gen. Gub. (Anordnungsblatt für den Kreis Petrikau Nr. 3/40) całkowity majątek żydowski podlega obowiązku zgłoszenia w terminie do dnia 10 marca r. b.

Odnośne urzędowe formularze, które w powyższym celu winien wypełnić każdy posiadając ... mający ukończone 21 lat, są do nabycia codz. w godz. 9 do 13 i od 15 do 17 do dnia 8 marca w lokalu Gminy (Garncarska 7)

Należycie wypełnione formularze winny być doręczone w lokalu przy ul. Garncarskiej 7 do dn. 10 marca r. b. w wyżej podanych godzinach.

Zarząd Gminy uprzedza wszystkich obowiązanych do zgłoszenia majątku, że wszelkie wykroczenia przeciwko wyżej wymienionemu rozporządzeniu podlegają karze więzienia i grzywny a majątki nie zgłoszone w terminie uważa się za bezpańskie i podlega konfiskacie.

Prezes Rady Starszych Gminy Żyd. w Piotrkowie.

Piotrków Trybunalski ghetto announcement from early 1940: "The Board of the Jewish Community in Piotrków informs that total declaration of Jewish property is subject to notification by 10 March 1940."

Leon Reichmann's first wife, Sala Jacobowitz Reichmann, c. 1941

Abek Brem, killed by the Nazis in a massacre of Jews on the outskirts of Piotrków Trybunalski, 1943

Two men with their Star of David armbands in September 1942, near the Piotrków Trybunalski military barracks, where two days later Jews were assembled for deportation

New identity: Gucia's photograph for her forged *Kennkarte*, in which she adopted the name Danuta Barbara Tanska, nicknamed "Basia"

Sabina Markowitz in Ulm, 1944

Barbara (right) and her surviving sister, Hela, at the Bergen-Belsen
Displaced Persons Camp, 1945

Barbara (center) and Sabina with other survivors at the Jewish Relief Center at the Deutsches Museum, Munich, fall 1945

Lau brothers Lulek (Yisrael) and Tulek (Naphtali) arriving in Haifa, Israel, 1945. Lulek holds the flag; Tulek is behind flag at far left. The flag says "Buchenwald" in Hebrew.

Barbara, Munich, 1946

Leon, Munich, 1946

Two of Barbara's brothers survived the Holocaust: Idek (left) and Josek (pictured with Barbara), Germany, 1946

Hela, Marek, and Jacob Brem, in Haifa, Israel, 1947

Barbara and Leon Reichmann, Munich, 1946

Henry Marton, Leon Reichmann's cousin and companion in the labor camps, survived and settled in Asbury Park, New Jersey

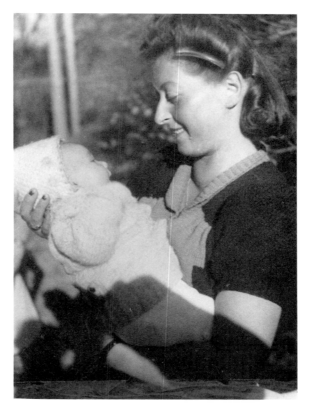

Barbara and Helen, Munich, November 1947

Barbara, Garmisch-Partenkirchen, Germany, 1948

Leon (top center) with other survivors at the dedication of a monument
commemorating victims of Bergen-Belsen Concentration Camp, 1948

Helen (age 2), Munich, 1949

Helen (age 10) and Henry (age 1),
Baltimore, Maryland, 1957

Barbara (age 52), Washington, DC, 1969

Barbara and Leon, Nevele Hotel, Kiamesha
Lake, New York, 1964

From Buchenwald to the
Vatican: Israeli Ambassador
Naphtali Lau-Lavie (left)
and Chief Rabbi of Israel,
Yisrael Meir Lau, with
Pope John Paul II, 1995

Barbara and Helen, Washington, DC, 1985

Barbara, 90th birthday celebration, Washington, DC, May 2006

Going Home

Alas!
Lonely sits the city
Once great with people!
She that was great among nations
Is become like a widow.
—Lamentations 1:1

NOVEMBER 1942

After nearly getting caught at the extermination company and my panicked flight from Nowy Sącz, I have been wandering around this small *Judenrein* tourist town of Rabka for a month, and I want to go home. I realize now how hard it would have been to hide in Piotrków and that the Polish woman who tricked me really did me a favor. At least here I've been able to move around freely and feel safe for the moment. How awful it would have been to be stuck in one small room, waiting for time to pass and feeling frightened with every sound.

But I can no longer stand this limbo and am ready to take the risk of going back to Piotrków.

My plan had been to disappear from the ghetto during the

deportations and then, after the month or so it would take for the Nazis to finish and move on to the next town, I would return. I am desperate to learn what has happened to my family and whether I still have a home to return to. I have had no news. The papers say nothing. There is no news at all. Well, no real news. Just that the Germans are winning and the British and the French and the Americans and the Soviets are weak and afraid and losing. There is no mention of Jews. There is no gossip in the streets. I can no longer stand the suspense and I am so bored.

I tell the owner of the guesthouse that I will be meeting some friends in Zakopane for the weekend and ask if I can leave my things with her. Arriving in Piotrków with a suitcase would draw attention, and I can carry a few essentials in my purse.

On my way to the train station, I walk through the park and notice a young woman sitting on a bench reading the paper. There is something very familiar about her, but I am in such a rush to find out about my family, I do not stop. I buy a ticket for Piotrków.

I get off the train and walk to the ghetto. It's pouring rain and cold and dark, which is fine. I don't want anyone to see me. I can't stop my shaking. I go to the main entrance of the ghetto and it is eerily quiet. There is no activity, no people rushing to and fro.

A huge Ukrainian standing guard there points his gun at me. "What do you want?" he barks.

I say, "A Jew owes me some money and I want it back."

"The Jews are gone and so is your money," he says.

I try to go in.

"And I will kill you if you come one step nearer."

I turn and go around to the back wall of the Christian cemetery. I can't get his words out of my head: "The Jews are gone."

I analyze his words, diagramming them like a grammar exercise in college. "The Jews"? All the Jews? "Gone"? Does that mean all gone? Do all the words mean the same in Ukrainian as in Polish?

I cross the cemetery and go to where the pig market used to be. As I knock on Kazimierz Dobranski's door, I feel torn between eagerness and dread to hear what news he may have for me. He opens the door; seeing me, his kind eyes fill with tears.

"Oh, Pani Gomolinska," he says gently. He hugs me and ushers me into the room.

I sit near the fire and he gives me some hot tea with a little sugar (where did he find that?).

We don't speak for a while. I don't want to hear what he is going to say and he doesn't want to say it. Finally, I tell him about what happened in Nowy Sącz and that I have been in Rabka. He says, "I think your brothers are all right. Josek and Idek. They are at the Dietrich and Fischer woodworking plant on the banks of the River Bugaj. The rabbi's son, Naphtali, and your cousin Elkanah are working at the glass factory at Hortensja. They are protected and safe because they are considered essential workers."

He looks at the floor. His voice goes flat. "Unfortunately, Milek didn't go to work on the day when they liquidated the ghetto."

"Liquidated?"

Pan Dobranski starts talking like a radio news reporter. He sounds like he is reading from a particularly uninteresting script.

"On October 13, the *Aktion* began. They picked up as many Jews as they could who had work cards and took them to their workplaces. Over the next two days the Nazis organized their information and started the deportations. They made all the Jews go to the Main Square, the Deportation Platz, and read from a list of names. The Nazis had forty old train cars, the ones they use for cattle, and they squeezed one hundred and fifty Jews into each one, six thousand altogether. If they

147

called your name you went, if not, you came back two days later. They had four transports of those trains, one every other day until October 21."

"That's twenty-four thousand people," I whisper.

"It was terrible," he says, tears in his eyes, still focused on the floor. "I saw it happening. The women, the children, the men, all being pushed and hit, forced into the cattle cars, stuffed in like sardines. I saw the sign on the cars. It said maximum six cows, or thirty-five people. The Nazis stuffed one hundred and fifty people into each car. There was no water, no food. Most cars didn't have toilets or even buckets. Some of the people threw photos and letters and rings through the small slats in the sidings. There were no windows and the doors were chained tight. I have some of their photos here."

He shows me, but neither of us recognizes the people.

"The last transport on October 21 was the cruelest. The Nazis realized that they didn't have six thousand names on the list and several of the cars were still empty. So they started rounding up people who thought they were secure and protected: the Jewish policemen, some of the tailors, those who had been promised they were important to the Reich. They say they have taken all those people to a concentration camp called Treblinka, near Malkinia. It is not a labor camp." Tears well up in his eyes and his hands are shaking. "They say the people are gassed immediately."

We sit silently, both staring at the floor. Then in a flat, monotone voice he continues. "After October 21, there were maybe two thousand 'legal' Jews left in the Little Ghetto. Those who had the work papers and are 'essential' are still working in the factories. We heard that after the *Aktion*, some Jews were able to stay hiding in the ghetto—in false ceilings and in cellars. But just last week the Nazis and the Ukrainians went through the ghetto knocking down ceilings and walls and they found people hiding, hundreds of them. The Ukrainians were even more brutal than the Nazis. They herded those poor people into the Great Synagogue, made them take off all of their clothes, and did horrible, inhumane things to them.

"My friend is a Polish policeman and came to tell me what he witnessed. I have never seen him so crazed or sick. He said that the Ukrainians kept the Jews in the synagogue for days, with no sanitation or water or food. Oh, Pani Gomolinska, how can people be so cruel to each other? The Ukrainians ripped the babies from their mothers' breasts and threw the infants against the walls. Then they threw their mangled little bodies into a huge bonfire. The mothers were screaming. The Ukrainians laughed and hooted as they shot the mothers while the milk flowed from their breasts. Then they loaded the living onto trucks."

Again, silence. He looks at me. "There are still a few fortunate Jews hiding outside the ghetto protected by Polish families. My place is so small," he says apologetically.

My mouth is filling with saliva. I am afraid I will throw up. I swallow the bitter bile down. I am afraid to look in his eyes.

"My father?" I ask.

"I'm so sorry," he says softly. "Your dear father and the two youngest were in the second transport to Treblinka."

"But not Regina? She was to be protected! We paid Pani Zbeingska with our silver candlesticks and furs and she promised to take Regina when the need came and dye her red hair brown."

He shakes his head no. "When the time came, Pani Zbeingska took the candlesticks and the furs but sent Regina back within one hour, still with her flaming-red hair, so all the world could see that she was a Jew. I'm so sorry," he says. "At least Regina was with her father and Beniek when the trains left."

"And Uncle Josef?"

"I don't know."

"And Hela and Marek?"

"I don't know. There was some story about Marek being taken to Bugaj hidden in a large sack."

"And Heniek?" I whisper. I am sure Heniek is fine. He was working for the *Judenrat* and must be more of an essential worker, even safer than being at Hortensja or Bugaj.

Pan Dobranski sadly shakes his head. "I don't know."

"And Rozia Nissenson?" But then he doesn't know who she is. "And the rabbi?"

"The rabbi was one of the last to go. I heard that he stood there while they beat him and they tried to humiliate him, but they could not break him. He was such a strong man, with his one arm. He said that he had to stay with his flock and he would not let them go alone like sheep to the slaughter. He told the Jews it was better to have a living death than a dead life. He was put on the last train."

"And Rebbitzin Lau and Lulek?"

"I don't know. I think they were able to hide," he says. "Pani Gomolinska, it is not safe for you here. They have not finished looking for Jews. You must go back to Rabka. I will walk with you to the train."

I have nothing to pay him with, no way to thank him. Soon I won't have enough money left to buy even my one bowl of soup. I feel totally numb like when Mama died, and again, I am moving like a robot. I am Gucia with no family left. Danuta Barbara is somewhere else. Somehow, we get to the station.

Then I start shaking through my core. My stomach feels numb and cold and hollow and sick, sick, sick, and my teeth are chattering. Pan Dobranski puts me on the train to Rabka.

The train goes through Kraków and I look out the window and remember taking this same journey on my way to begin university, when

I was young and innocent and happy, to meet my future. Was it only a few years ago? How can the scenery look unchanged when the universe bears no resemblance to what it was? I remember that time, looking forward to exploring new parts of Poland if I wasn't too busy with my studies. In fact, Itka Moskowitz and I had talked of visiting Oświęcim sometime to see the sights; it was a picturesque market town fifty kilometers south of Kraków. Of the twelve thousand people living there, seven thousand were Jews whose ancestors had lived there for over five hundred years. There were even twelve synagogues in that little town. We were also curious to see the Gypsies, who seemed fascinating and exotic in our imaginations. Now, in this new universe, this town of Oświęcim, which the Germans call Auschwitz, is not only *Judenrein* but "cleansed" of the hated Gypsies as well. It is not a destination I would choose for a pleasure trip.

For weeks I have controlled my emotions every moment. But now I cannot control myself. I have used up all my strength or will to go on.

I sob the many hours on the train, hoping no one will notice. Perhaps they will just think I have a very bad cold.

Sabina

For wherever you go, I will go;
wherever you lodge, I will lodge;
Your people shall be my people,
and your God my God.
—Ruth 1:16

DECEMBER 1942

I cannot believe that I have slept, dreamlessly, through the night. I awake in my small bed in my guesthouse in Rabka and I think of what Pan Dobranski has told me. Maybe Idek and Josek and Hela and Marek are safe. But my father and Beniek and Regina and the rabbi and twenty-four thousand of my *landsmen*. Are they dead or being tortured or are they just working in some other place? How can any of this be true?

I have no idea what to do. I have no plan and no hope. I get up like a brainless machine and wash and dress and leave the room and walk to a café and have coffee and buy the newspaper and walk to the park.

Sitting on that same bench is the young woman I saw as I was leaving for Piotrków. I look at her and realize I know her. It is Sabina Sheratska; Markowitz before she married. I recognize her from Piotrków.

We never really knew each other, but I remember that night so long ago, when she and her friends Leon Reichmann and Henry Marton and Sala Jacobowitz and others in Betar mocked David Ben-Gurion. I remember that big fight and how horrified I was that Jews would be so violent with each other. It would be safer for me to walk on, not take a chance of arousing suspicion, but I feel so lonely and desperate. I take the risk and sit next to her on the bench. In a whisper, in Polish, we start to talk.

I tell Sabina all the heartbreaking news that I have just learned from Pan Dobranski and she sits there, stunned like me. She and her husband had escaped from the ghetto separately, since it would be more dangerous for her to be with a Jewish man if they were stopped. He is living with a Pole outside Warsaw and they have been able to stay in touch by mail. We decide to share a room. It will save both of us money and at least we won't be alone anymore.

We stay in Rabka for a few weeks. Luckily for Sabina her husband is very well off and has good contacts. He is able to send her money each month, so unlike me she does not suffer constant hunger. It is difficult to sit across from her at a restaurant, sipping my meager bowl of soup, while Sabina can afford a real meal; but I understand that in these times no one knows how long they will have to stretch their limited resources. And from earliest childhood Sabina has been sickly, so she must eat enough to maintain her strength.

Even more important, her husband has been able to send her an official *Kennkarte*, the German identification card. Hers is foolproof. Sabina has dark, wavy brown hair but bright blue eyes and her Polish is perfect, so with her valid *Kennkarte* she feels safe that she can pass.

The name she has chosen for herself is Janina, Junka for short, and that is what I will call her. I tell her to call me Basia. She is worried sick about her family and, like me, driven to despair by the loneliness and boredom.

Because of her, Sabina's husband helps me, too. He instructs me to have a regulation-size photo taken and to send it to him. He uses the photo I have mailed to him and he sends me back an authentic government *Kennkarte* with my new name and my picture stamped with the official German seal. Once I add my fingerprints, it's perfect! So much better than my barely passable ghetto forgery. This is more important than food!

In order to better pass as gentile Poles, we decide to go to the Catholic church to familiarize ourselves with what they do. We sit in the back and watch the strange ceremonies. We try to mimic the motions of the people sitting in front of us. It is so difficult because the service is in Latin and what little I remember of the basic vocabulary and grammar I learned in school does me no good here at all. We don't understand a word. But we go home and practice crossing ourselves and wonder what that small *matzo* they put on the people's tongues must taste like.

We have heard that there are still a few Jews hiding in Rabka and the Gestapo is looking for them, so we decide to leave and go to Zakopane. It is another resort town and we will just be carefree Polish tourists on our Christmas holidays in the Tatra Mountains with no thoughts of the war.

Into the Lions' Den

Daniel was then brought and thrown into the lions' den.
The king spoke to Daniel and said: "Your God, whom
you serve so regularly, will deliver you."
—Daniel 6:16

FEBRUARY 1943

Zakopane is truly beautiful but bitingly cold. Sabina and I have the same boring routine each day. We wake up, have coffee, read the paper, go to another café for coffee, take a walk, go back to our room to rest, find a cheap restaurant for dinner. Sabina orders a small meal. I have just a bowl of soup. We try to fortify ourselves from the icy weather. I am worrying about money and Sabina is worrying about her husband. She has enough money to last her for a while, but she has not heard from him for six weeks.

APRIL 1943

I am almost out of money and must find work. We don't talk about it much, but we are both worried that Sabina's husband has been caught.

We know that the Nazis urgently need workers for menial labor in Germany and are conscripting Poles to work there. Those Poles who can afford it pay lower-class Poles to go in their place. Few, but some, volunteer. I know that we can find jobs easily here in Poland but even so, we are not safe in Zakopane for a minute.

My mama always said that a Pole could smell a Jew a mile away, and that is true. Each day we are here is a danger and we are both on edge. I suggest to Sabina that we go to the *Arbeitsampt*, the German employment bureau, and volunteer to work as maids in Germany. That way we can make money and work in a private home, away from prying eyes. The irony is startling. We would be safer in Germany than here.

The Germans' blind submission to authority makes them stupid. If the government says there are no more Jews left in Germany, they could be looking one in the eye and not believe that person could be a Jew. Here a Pole might see a Jew; there a German would only see a Pole.

But Sabina is afraid. She can afford to keep moving from town to town, and she worries she doesn't have the stamina for physical labor. She suffered from tuberculosis as a child and has always been frail. And of course there would be the danger of exposing ourselves to scrutiny at the *Arbeitsampt*.

Even though I dread the prospect of being on my own again, I don't see that I have a choice. Unlike Sabina, I have to earn some money soon to keep from starving. And after almost getting caught at the extermination company in Nowy Sącz, I know it is too dangerous to take a job in Poland. So I dress like a Polish peasant, pinch my cheeks to look healthy, and with my heart in my throat and my *Kennkarte* in my purse, I go to present myself to the local *Arbeitsampt*.

Fortunately the intake worker is a *Volksdeutsche*. This German woman speaks Polish poorly, so she has no idea that my accent is educated and not that of a peasant. It all goes quickly and smoothly and after typing up my registration she tells me to report to the transition camp in Kraków on Friday. I go back to the room feeling sad to be separating from Sabina but mostly relieved that I passed.

But Sabina has had a change of heart. While I was gone she realized how terrified she was of going our separate ways.

"Basia," she says, "I would rather risk my physical health with hard labor than my sanity from being alone again. And now seeing that you made it through, I want to go tomorrow to apply as well. Please, will you come with me?"

I am shaken by her request. This means exposing myself to danger again for no reason. She shouldn't have put me in that difficult position, but I cannot say no. So on Tuesday I go with her—again into the lions' den.

The woman stares at Sabina. "I don't know about you. You look like you could be a Jew," she says.

"With those blue eyes?" I snap.

The woman says that the other day they almost caught a Jew. But the Jew escaped by jumping through a window, breaking the glass, and leaving blood everywhere.

We look at her blankly.

"Well, it is a good *Kennkarte*," the woman says, looking at Sabina's identification papers, and she stamps her registration.

It is done. Sabina and I are happy! We are going to Germany!

Friday, Sabina and I report to the transit camp in Kraków. We are in a group of a thousand Polish registered workers. Both of us are in a panic and barely talk at all, so afraid of giving something away. Can they tell that we are Jews? Can they tell from our accents that we are educated city girls and not uneducated villagers? We are herded into a large, now-empty factory which has been turned into a dormitory and we each get a little cot. We feel lucky to get the ones by the wall. All of the women must sleep together in that one huge room. But first we are called to dinner in another vast room. None of us has eaten any food all day and we are starving.

We are each given a bowl and stand in line. A huge vat is steaming. They give us some black bread and then ladle something that looks like goulash into the bowl: hot meat swimming in a thick soup. It smells delicious. The serving is generous, and the bread is not too coarse. We sit at large tables, surrounded by maybe eight hundred Polish women. Some of the women cross themselves and mutter a short prayer before they eat, so we do, too. With the first spoonful, Sabina and I glance furtively at each other. We realize that this meat is pork. If we hesitate, if we do not eat it, we will be discovered. And if one of us does not eat it, both of us will be found out. I cross myself again and bow my head, and silently I recite the Shema, our holiest prayer: *"Sh'ma Yis'ra'eil Adonai Eloheinu Adonai Echad"* (Hear, O Israel, the Lord is our God, the Lord is One). What else can we do? In Jewish law, life is holy, and the preservation of life—one's own as well as the lives of others—is our highest command-ment, more important than almost any other *mitzvah*. So in this mo-ment, because our lives depend on it, we must eat non-kosher food.

The woman sitting at the next chair looks at me curiously.

"I have not had meat in so long," I whisper. "I had to thank Mother Mary before I ate more."

The pork is delicious and both Sabina and I take the dark bread and wipe our bowls clean. I can't tell if I am relieved, surprised, disgusted, or ashamed. I have been hungry for so long.

It is lights out and, like most of the other women in our dormitory, Sabina and I kneel at our beds, cross ourselves, and pray before we get under the covers. The truth is we are actually praying to any God who will listen.

The next day is Saturday, our Shabbos. We are given eggs and bacon for breakfast. Again we eat. Again it is delicious. Then we are forced to remove all of our clothes, put them on top of our suitcases and walk, totally naked, into a large shower room, leaving our suitcases and clothes on the side, near the walls, where we can keep an eye on them. Cold water comes flowing out of the showerheads and we are told to lather ourselves with the harsh soap. I have never stood unclothed in front of anyone in my life. I feel utterly humiliated. I keep my eyes closed tight.

We are given rags to dry ourselves and then they spray us with powder, I suppose to kill any lice. Still naked, we stand in a line and we are examined, everywhere, in every little private place of our bodies, by male doctors. It is a disgusting and traumatic experience. But I keep thinking how lucky Sabina and I are to be women. If we were Jewish men, the physical mark of our covenant with God would mean immediate discovery and death.

After that degrading examination, we are allowed to put our clothes back on and then we take our suitcases and are marched to the train station and put back on the trains. We are two Jews who are escaping from the Nazis and this evil war by choosing to go to Nazi Germany.

For the first time in so long, much to my surprise, I feel relief. The trains are very nice. Sabina and I are able to sit next to each other on comfortable seats. We start to relax. We are allowed to choose our destination and are aiming to get to the most southwest part of Germany, near the Swiss border. My heart flutters when we cross the old border from what was once my beloved Poland into Germany, though it could be said that we had already been living in Germany since October 6, 1939, when Hitler declared victory in Poland.

But my relief is short-lived. An SS officer, whom I'd noticed looking our way, takes the unoccupied seat on my other side. He asks if we speak German, and I say that I do. After some inane small talk he asks what kind of work we are looking for. In my very best German I tell him we both want to work as a *Wirtschaft*, thinking that it means domestic maid in a private house. Sabina and I hope to stay together, but we know that it might not be possible, and perhaps we would be safer apart. If one of us gets caught the other might still be free. And I reason that if we work in private houses we can keep to ourselves; the fewer people we are in contact with, the better. It seems the safest option.

But my German isn't as good as I think. I should have said *Wirtschafterin*, housekeeper. Instead, by answering *Wirtschaft* I am unintentionally asking for housekeeping work as a chambermaid in a hotel.

The SS man's eyes light up. "*Ach, wunderbar!* I have a friend in Ulm who needs two *Wirtschaft*s."

Even though Ulm is quite a distance from the Swiss border, we are too exhausted to travel farther, and are thrilled for the chance to stay together, so we agree.

We get off the train with mostly women because so many of the Polish young men have already been taken as prisoners or forced laborers. Waiting at the station are hundreds of fat, well-dressed German men looking us over the way my *tatte* would look at the cows before buying the choicest ones to be slaughtered. A farmer immediately points at me, commenting on my healthy red cheeks, then examining my teeth.

But the SS man says, "No! She is already taken," and then he waves to a man in the crowd.

We are introduced to Sigmund Schweibold, the owner of the Gasthaus zum Rotter Lowen. He is very happy to see the SS man and seems quite pleased with Sabina and me. We go to his hotel and restaurant and he takes us up to our room. We cannot believe our luck. The room is actually quite nice and again we feel relieved. It is on the top floor in a finished attic. We have a spacious room with three beds and our very own toilet and bath.

But in a moment our relief turns to panic. We learn that a Polish woman, Marysa, occupies the third bed; she will be working with us. We have come to Germany to escape the prying eyes of the Poles, and now we will be spending each day and night with one. What will happen to us if we cry out in Yiddish in our sleep?

Sabina and I are not quite sure if it is praying to our God of Abraham, Isaac, and Jacob, or kneeling and crossing ourselves and praying to the mother of a Jewish rabbi named Jesus, but three weeks later the owner's wife discovers that Marysa is pregnant and has her immediately sent back to Poland.

Unlike her husband, Frau Schweibold is an ardent member of the Nazi party, but she doesn't seem to have any doubts about Sabina and me. Now we have the bedroom all to ourselves. We are surrounded by unsuspecting Germans, and for the first time since September 1, 1939, we can take deep breaths and relax from most of our fears. There is a regular rhythm to the days and we settle in to a blessedly busy, boring, and safe routine.

One of my jobs is to serve breakfast—a lowly Pole would never be allowed to serve lunch or dinner. Plus I must remove the dirty dishes from the tables and clean the rooms. Then for the rest of the afternoon and into the evening I wash and cut the food and help in the kitchen. Sabina works all day cooking, and she is a very good cook.

The restaurant is famous for its potato salad. My job in the kitchen is to wash and boil the potatoes and then, when the potatoes have cooled, remove the skins and dice them. One might think I would soon get sick of potatoes, but I am so skinny and have been so hungry for four years that I eat as much as I dice. It is "one for the pot, one for Basia, one for the pot, one for Basia."

A month after being here, as I am sweeping the second floor, I see the SS man from the train come into the lobby. I overhear him ask Frau Schweibold for the pretty blond Polish girl.

But she doesn't want him distracting me from my work and gets rid of him. "She's very busy right now. I can't possibly interrupt her from her work. But I'll let her know you were here. Goodbye!"

I suppose he had more in mind than simply being helpful when he got us these jobs. Fortunately he doesn't return.

The next morning, as I am serving breakfast, a German soldier looks at my yellow armband with the *P* that shows I am a Polish worker and then smiles and winks at me. He says, "There must be some mistake, Fräulein. You can't possibly be Polish." For a moment, my heart stops. "You look so German and you speak so well." I relax, smile back, and quickly go into the kitchen. Such a warm feeling of safety is flooding over me, a marvelous sense of security I have not felt since the war began. I look German. They think I am Polish. They have no idea that I am a Jew.

There is another worker at the hotel. A German girl, thank God. Her name is Maya and she lives with her parents on the outskirts of Ulm. She comes every day at nine a.m. and leaves by ten p.m. It is Maya who is fit to serve the German guests their lunch and dinner. Maya is a lovely young woman and always smells so good. She says her cologne is called Heliotrope and it has the same sweet scent as that fragile purple flower. Sabina is a few years older than I, but Maya and I are exactly the same age and temperament. We get along very well.

JUNE 1943

I am getting fat from eating all those potatoes, so I decide to go on a diet. When I decide on a course of action, I don't do things halfway. That is how I've always been. So I limit my eating very strictly. I guess this is too big a shock to my system, because my monthly periods stop. This worries me and I ask Frau Schweibold if she thinks this is a serious problem.

What worries Frau Schweibold is that she might have another pregnant Pole on her hands whom she will have to send back. She takes me to a doctor, and even though I know I can't be pregnant I am still nervous that he might find something and she could send me back to Poland. But moments after examining me the doctor tells me to dress and return to the reception area.

With an amused expression on his face he addresses Frau Schweibold—right in front of me—and says, "There is no need to consult the laboratory for a diagnosis in this case. Fräulein Tanska cannot be pregnant because she is still a virgin." And the doctor tells me to gain some weight.

It registers with me that I have enough food to eat and I have been worrying about getting fat instead of worrying about starving to death. After four years of fear and depression and fighting for my life or drifting in numb detachment, I am now secure in my daily routine, the constant supply of good food, and the certain belief that sooner or later the Americans will destroy the Nazi regime and end this horror. My work keeps me too busy to think. I live in the moment. And I am shocked to realize that I am actually happy in Ulm.

On Tuesdays Sabina and I have a half day off. After cleaning the restaurant and the hotel rooms, we often walk along the banks of the Danube River and go to a movie. Sometimes we wander to the magnificent Ulm Münster, their fourteenth-century Gothic cathedral with (they tell us) the world's tallest church steeple. We sit in the back during evening service, looking at the wooden carvings, listening to the music, and practicing being Catholic. Every now and then we stand outside the old fourteenth-century *Rathaus*, the town hall, looking at the astronomical clock as it slowly counts the minutes and hours.

Three or four times a week we have to set an alarm to wake us at two a.m. so we can let the soldiers out to catch the three a.m. train. Because of the war and security, the front door of the hotel is locked overnight so that guests cannot leave unless one of us unlocks the door. Herr Schweibold has a contract with the Wehrmacht that makes his business very profitable. The soldiers get a room at the hotel, eat dinner, get drunk, sing their patriotic "Heil Hitler" and "Deutschland über alles" songs, get a little sleep, and then leave after we open the door in time for them to catch their train.

After six months of working hard all day every day and then getting up at two in the morning several times a week, Sabina and I are exhausted.

Maybe it's reckless to challenge the boss when he could have me sent back to Poland in an instant, but I just can't take being exploited like this anymore. We presented ourselves as workers, not slaves. I tell Herr Schweibold that I am just not able to go on like this and if I can't get more sleep then I will have to find another job.

"Don't worry," he says. "Nobody wants that. My wife and I will alternate nights with you and Junka, and you will be able to get your rest."

But after trying this for a little while, Herr Schweibold decides the extra money isn't worth losing his sleep or losing us. He tells any guests checking in that they have to stay until the morning, and now we all sleep through the night and everyone is in a better mood.

As soon as summer comes I can't wait to sunbathe. I have always been addicted to the sun. Now I spend each *Zimmerstunde*, our two-hour lunch break, on the banks of the Danube. Sabina stays in our room. She is not interested in making her skin darker.

The first time I walk along the river I see a mother duck followed by her six ducklings, and I have to hold back tears. What a surprise to feel such depths of emotion—I have kept my feelings suppressed for so long. But it reminds me of my family and of how every Shabbos, after our midday meal, my mother would take all of us to visit Uncle Josef and Tante Sura. Mama would lead, holding the baby and the next youngest by the hand, then two by two the rest of us would follow, just like those ducks. The jagged knife of reality plunges deep into my heart. The Mama I remember and most of those happy little ducks are dead. Will I ever wake up from this nightmare?

One day, as I am sunning myself by the river, two SS men approach me and ask for my identification papers. I answer that I left the papers at home. As usual, when I leave the hotel, I don't wear my yellow armband identifying myself as a Pole. The last thing I want is to attract the attention of any Poles living in Ulm.

"Where are you from?" one of the SS asks gruffly.

"Poland," I answer.

"Don't you know you must always wear your armband whenever you go out?" he snaps.

With no time to carefully choose my words, I snap back as if affronted, "I didn't think I'd have to wear it when I'm half-naked. It would ruin my suntan!"

The two men laugh and relax. "Well, from now on wear your armband," one of them says, and they walk away. It is only then that I feel afraid, and I shiver lying there in the bright sun.

I remember the time I went with Sabina to register for work at the *Arbeitsampt* when the *Volksdeutsche* signing us up suspected Sabina of being a Jew. Then, too, looking the woman straight in the eyes, I operated on instinct. I acted like I thought her question was stupid and snapped back at her. Remembering that, I start to feel the warmth of the sun and I am relieved to realize that when it comes to saving my life, Basia is more brazen and quick on her feet than Gucia could ever have been.

AUGUST 1943

I use the address that Uncle Josef gave me for my cousin Janek in Poland. I write to him as Basia and, carefully choosing my words, tell him only of my good fortune to be working for the wonderful Germans and that I have a job in Ulm. I soon get a letter back. We are very discreet and write often, trying to sound the way Poles would speak. At one point Janek asks me to send him two pairs of used work boots for my two brothers and it gives me hope that Josek and Idek are still alive, but I worry about their situation. Before, even when they were doing forced labor at Bugaj, Idek and Josek always had clothes on their backs and shoes on their feet. What kind of conditions could they be living in now that they would need old work boots? I send the boots and also some fresh apples. Janek later writes to thank me for the boots, with no mention of the apples. They must have been stolen at the post office.

SEPTEMBER 1943

A car horn is blaring in the driveway. Herr Schweibold goes running out of the lobby, down the stairs. I peek out the kitchen window to see a large, rotund German man getting out of a black Mercedes. He is tall and well-dressed, with a large black mustache like a walrus and a mop of black hair on his head. He rushes to Herr Schweibold and they warmly hug each other, talking, talking, talking. He goes back to his car and takes out a suitcase and a briefcase, and arm in arm they walk up the stairs into the lobby.

"Basia," Herr Schweibold calls to me.

I come from the kitchen, quickly swallowing the potato in my mouth and drying my hands on a kitchen towel.

"Basia. Here is Uncle Fritz. He is our most special guest."

And when he says the word *special*, his left eyebrow goes up and his right eyebrow goes down. "Uncle Fritz will be staying with us for a few days and he will want his coffee hot and black at exactly 7:40 tomorrow morning. Of course you will clean his room spotlessly, as you always do," he says to me very intently.

"Junka," he bellows, and Sabina comes running from the kitchen. "Junka, this is our Uncle Fritz and he is our most special guest. He will absolutely love your apple pancakes. Be sure they are ready for him at eight tomorrow morning." And they go off, arm in arm, chatting, into the library.

I get up extra-early to be sure that the coffee I make for Uncle Fritz is hot and black, but not as black as the coffee I made for Heniek and my friends from Hashomer Hatsair (where are they now?). I am surprised to see that Maya is in the kitchen and the water is already boiling. I wonder what this means. She lives so far away; there is no way she could have gotten here so early. She barely looks at me.

At nine o'clock I clean Uncle Fritz's room. There is a faint smell of heliotrope perfume in the air.

Uncle Fritz comes every few weeks. Some of those times Maya climbs into bed with me in the middle of the night. She is disgusted that Uncle Fritz is unable "to perform" and so she leaves him snoring in his bed.

MAY 1944

Sabina and I have been in Germany for more than a year. We are safe and full of food. We heard that before the war there were only five hundred Jews living in all of Ulm. Of course they and the synagogue are long gone. But this fact, that there were hardly any Jews in the city, makes us feel even safer. The people in Ulm do not know what a Jew is. Sabina and I are so busy each day that we have no time to think about anything besides what we are doing. This life is so simple. Our only decisions are what to do during our lunch break and on our half day off each week. We give the boss our tips because we don't have enough free time to spend even our measly wages. And we are sure that after the war the deutschmark will be worthless. The fact is, even though we are often exhausted, we have become used to our lives and are even, I have to admit, generally content.

But as safe as we feel, we yearn to know when the world will return to normal. I read the newspapers every day and know that the German words are lies. I know that the Americans are strong and that they will defeat the Nazis, but how much longer will it take?

The Allies are now starting to bomb Germany. We have had a few bombings already in Ulm. Maya sometimes spends nights at the hotel, not wanting to be out after dark.

JUNE 1944

The night bombings have become more and more intense. The siren blows and we wake up and struggle out of bed, grab our suitcases, and run down to the cellar. Then at dawn we go to work. Some nights we are so exhausted we don't even bother to get up but just sleep through the air raid.

JULY 1944

It is the middle of the night. A siren blares and we wake up. Sabina and I decide to stay in bed. We've spent so many nights needlessly awake in the cellar when nothing ever happened. But this time Herr Schweibold is pounding on our door. He insists we go to the cellar *now*! The planes are very close.

Huddled down in the cellar, we hear them directly overhead. There is a tremendous crash, an explosion, and the ceiling of the cellar is raining pieces of plaster on our heads. And then, FIRE! Fire everywhere, smoke and plaster and screaming and running and I grab my suitcase and I can't see or breathe and someone grabs my hand and coughing and choking we run to the outside. We run and run and there are bombs exploding and fire everywhere. There is no moon and the only light is from the fires that are burning through the streets of Ulm.

It is Maya who has grabbed my hand. She yells that we must run to her family's house outside the city.

But Sabina. Where is Sabina?

I panic. I run off searching for her. I scream for her in Polish, in German, and without thinking, in Yiddish.

I scream: "Junka!" and "Sabina!" and "Sabineleh!" but she is nowhere. Maya runs after me and again grabs my hand and pulls me along.

Losing Sabina

Two are better than one, because they have a good reward for their
toil. For if they fall, one will lift up his fellow.
But woe to him who is alone when he falls and
has not another to lift him up!
—Ecclesiastes 4:9–10

JULY 1944

We run through the night, two young, frightened girls running from
Death. I don't know how long we run but after a while we outrun the
chaos and arrive at Maya's home.

Maya's parents are overwhelmed with relief to see her. They are kind
and openhearted people. Maya has spoken nicely of me and they tell
me that I am welcome to stay with them as a member of the family.
They are poor but they treat me like a daughter and share their food
with me, even though I am a Pole.

I stay here for a month, helping as much as I can with the housework
and food preparation each day. Then one night I am awakened from
my sleep by someone climbing onto the cot where I sleep. It is Maya's
father. He whispers in my ear that I must not say a word, that I owe

them for the food and the shelter, that he will make me very happy. I am frightened, but even more outraged. I kick him hard and slap him in the face and run to the outhouse, where I lock myself in until dawn. Then I sneak into the house to grab my suitcase and walk back to Ulm. I know the hotel is closed, nearly demolished the night of the bombing, so I go straight to the *Arbeitsampt*, where I am first in line. I tell them I have lost my job because of the bombing and need new work. I ask if they have a record of my cousin, Janina Sieracka, whom I lost during the bombing, but they say no.

They send me to a restaurant on the other side of Ulm. The place is absolutely filthy. I have a small room the size of a closet, but it has a bolt on the door, so no one can get into my bed. My job is similar to what it was at the Gasthaus zum Rotter Lowen. I peel potatoes and peel potatoes and peel potatoes.

Then one day I cut my left thumb badly. It does not heal but becomes red and swollen and throbs all night and the nail looks strange. After two weeks I can't stand the pain anymore and go to a doctor. He tells me that I have a serious infection and might lose my thumb. He operates on it and I am sent to recover at a clinic for foreign workers run by the Catholic Church, with a special barracks for Poles. My worst nightmare, to be with Poles.

I am so afraid that in my fever I might say something in Yiddish or call out "Mamashi." I don't, but I know they suspect me anyway. They know from the way I speak Polish that I am not a peasant girl.

When my fever is gone and I can get out of bed, some of the Polish girls follow me to the chapel and insist I go first to take Holy Communion. Even though Sabina and I had observed the Mass, I had never taken Communion before and am terrified I will look awkward and give myself away. I kneel and cross myself and open my mouth and the priest puts something like *matzo* on my tongue. The wine has the same sweet taste as the wine we drink at Passover. The Polish girls say nothing and I am able to breathe again.

Now that I am up and out of bed, the nun takes advantage of my fluency in German and has me help with simple chores and errands. I am happy to help. She is a kind woman and I am glad for an escape from the Poles. Whenever the doctor asks about my progress she tells him I need more time to heal. I think she may suspect I am a Jew and wishes to protect me, because she keeps me there for another two weeks even after I am well enough to go back to work. But finally I must leave.

I return to the *Arbeitsampt*. I ask again if they have a record of a Janina Sieracka, and this time they do! She is working at an inn in Lindau on Lake Constance, near the Swiss border. I tell them she is my cousin, that we had worked together at the Gasthaus zum Rotter Lowen and we were bombed and separated and could I be sent to Lindau and work in the same place and they say yes.

SEPTEMBER 1944

I get off the train in Lindau and buy a small bunch of flowers at the train station. What a beautiful city, a small peaceful resort surrounded by a lake and so near the Swiss border. I ask for directions to the Hotel am Holdereggenpark and walk the three kilometers, my heart pounding with anticipation.

The restaurant looks lovely, clean, and neat and I walk directly into the kitchen and there she is. And we hug forever and we laugh and we cry. I feel as if I am home. Sabina and I are together and safe and working, but everything is now rationed and we are hungry again. We have only one meal a day, *Stamgerickt*. It is potatoes and vegetables and we can have as much as we want, but after the marvelous meals in Ulm, it is practically tasteless.

DECEMBER 1944

It is just dawn. It is still dark and very cold but there is a bright full moon shining through the window. The alarm has not yet rung but something wakes me up. In the faint light of the moon I see Sabina sitting up in her bed, her eyes wide open. She looks stunned, like she's in shock.

"Sabina," I whisper, "are you okay?"

"I've just had the strangest dream, Basia," she says in a hoarse, monotone voice. "It was so clear. It was so real. My mother came to me and woke me up. She said 'Sabina, I am dead. Your father is dead. Your husband is dead. There is nothing you can do about it. Gone is gone. But soon the war will be over, and Sabina, don't be sad because Leon Reichmann is still alive. Go and find him. I love you, *meine maidele.*' And she kissed me and disappeared. That's when I woke up. I think it was a few hours ago. It was so real. I felt her kiss." And she points to her forehead.

I go to her bed and hug her. She is trembling, and not from the cold. I hold her tightly, to keep her from blowing away.

APRIL 13, 1945

A guest at the restaurant reads from the newspaper to announce that the president of the United States, Franklin Delano Roosevelt, died yesterday, and everyone stands up and cheers. They are exultant, sure that now the Germans will certainly win the war. But I know that isn't true. America is strong, and it is just a matter of time.

Liberation

After the final destruction of Nazi tyranny, they hope to see
established a peace which will afford to all nations the means
of dwelling in safety within their own boundaries, and which
will afford assurance that all the men in all the lands may live
out their lives in freedom from fear and want.
—Franklin D. Roosevelt (1882–1945) and
Winston Churchill (1874–1965),
Atlantic Charter, August 1941

MAY 5, 1945

I am cleaning the restaurant after the lunchtime crowd when a group of Algerian soldiers from a unit in the French army comes barging in. They are smiling and laughing and we do not need to know French to understand the meaning of the word they are shouting: *"Libération!"*

Sabina comes running from the kitchen.

The Allies have won the war. The Germans have lost, surrendered. It's over!

Sabina and I are free. Free!

The soldiers tell us, in French and broken German and broken

English that now we Poles can take whatever we want from the *Schwein*. They say to go plunder because we are now the victors. Go to all the stores and just take. But we are not that hungry and the shop-keepers are not our enemies. We really don't need anything except our pasts returned to us. Our dead families and friends, our innocence, our youth.

There will be a big party tonight. The soldiers invite us to go, and to dance and sing and get drunk. Sabina enthusiastically wants to go, but I need to sit quietly alone and digest what all this means.

Five years of fear and hiding and loss. What will we do now? Where will we go? What will we find? And dare we tell anyone that we are Jews?

The soldiers ask me what I want to drink. They offer me wine, champagne, vodka, vermouth. Except for the wine on Passover, I have never drunk alcohol. I tell them vermouth because the sound of the word feels so beautiful in my mouth. They bring me a bottle and Sabina goes to the dance with them. I sit in my room and drink the whole bottle of vermouth, thinking about my past and wondering about my future.

(I have never been sicker in my life than that following morning, that whole day, that night. Even on the boat to America, I was not as sick as on that glorious day of Liberation. And that is why ever since then I have refused even a sip of alcohol, except at Passover or when joining in a toast on festive occasions like bar mitzvahs and weddings.)

MAY 7, 1945

We are free, liberated. We should be joyful, but are we safe? We are so far from home. And where is home? The Algerian soldiers take us to a transport formed to take the Polish workers back to Poland. We still do not dare tell anyone that we are Jews. We travel all day crowded in dirty trucks, pushed against dirty, smelly bodies, our own sweat adding to the overall stench.

We are bumped and jostled over rough, bombed roads and we are told that this night we will sleep in a now-vacant German officers' barracks. After the crowding of the trucks, it sounds like a luxury, as there will be three cots for three people to each room.

At sunset, aching, exhausted, thirsty, and famished, and desperately needing a toilet, we get off the transport with all the Poles. First, after using the smelly toilets and happy to have them, we go to a large mess hall and the food is that same horrible watery potato soup, so like the kind I used to make in Piotrków in the ghetto. Sabina and I still cross ourselves and pretend to pray. The war is over but we are surrounded by Poles who might hate the Jews. We eat and are happy for whatever that black liquid is that they are calling coffee.

When we go to our assigned room we see that the other bed is already taken. There is a woman lying on her stomach sobbing her heart out. Sabina and I go over to her and gently touch her back.

"Can we help?" we whisper in Polish.

She turns over and I gasp. It is Mania Wajshof, Heniek's younger sister!

No, is it possible? She sits up and we hug and cry and cannot get over the coincidence. I have not seen Mania for five long, painful years. I worry because her sister Dora is not there. And Mania is crying so violently.

I am afraid to ask, but I must. "Your family?"

"Gone," she sobs, "all gone." She hugs me again, fresh tears flowing. "Oh, Gucia, I am so sorry. I know that you had broken up with Heniek, but all those precious years you had together. We were all taken in the third transport to Treblinka. Only I survived."

I am not surprised, but not knowing the truth about Heniek had helped me get through the years. I would think of him so often: the good times we had when we were younger—perhaps the chance of meeting again after the war; perhaps I would feel different this time.

"After you and he separated, he was heartbroken," Mania says. "But then he met a very nice girl from near Łódź, Maryla Planska. Heniek became a Jewish policeman because he thought that would make him more protected and secure. They were married in late September, just before the *Aktion*."

I feel shocked and embarrassed at my sudden emotion. It's true, I was the one who chose to break up with Heniek, and yet I feel such a deep pang of jealousy, and I am horribly ashamed.

Mania is sobbing again and so am I.

"We were all standing together in the Deportation Platz as Nazis read names from their lists. They called out all of our names, but for some reason they didn't call Maryla. But Maryla chose to go anyway. She said her life was worth nothing without Heniek."

I can barely breathe. There is a tight band around my chest and my heart is pounding violently. And if I had married Heniek? If I had not refused him in my search for true love? If we had run away to Russia like he had planned, would he be alive today? If Maryla had not gone with Heniek, would she be alive today? I hope I will never, ever have to make a choice like that again. I am shaking and I feel so very, very sick.

Mania buries her head in the pillow and weeps. Sabina and I hug each other thinking of our escape from Piotrków and the bombing in Ulm and we realize how very lucky we are.

We have been traveling in the transport for several days. Each day is the same. We are squeezed in like sardines, smelly, thirsty, hungry, black-and-blue from the bumping on the rough roads. But there are no bombs and no Nazis and often we all break out in song and tell jokes and stories.

This night we are separated from Mania, because this nicer barracks, used by high-ranking German officers, has only two cots in each room. It's an odd arrangement. Sabina and I are placed in a small room with a connecting door to a room where two men will sleep.

It is the middle of the night and we hear loud, drunken voices. It is a couple of Algerian soldiers looking for women. They pound on our door and Sabina and I quickly move our two cots against it. We unlock the connecting door and rush into the room of the two Polish men and get into their beds, hoping that they are the lesser danger.

"Please, please protect us. Please say we are your wives," we plead. Mercifully, they do what we ask and yell out to the Algerians, who then leave us alone.

May 12, 1945

Mania is eager to return to Piotrków, but Sabina and I are not ready to go back now, if ever. And we no longer feel safe traveling with the Algerian transport. But where to go instead? Then we hear that there are a lot of Jews in Munich, more coming each day. After hugging Mania with a teary goodbye, Sabina and I leave the transport and hitchhike the rest of the way to Munich. It's not hard to get rides since there are so many American soldiers on the roads; American trucks are constantly going back and forth. The Americans are very nice to us. They tell us that they are not supposed to pick us up but they do it anyway and give us chocolate and cigarettes. They laugh and say we are fat enough to eat the chocolate. We don't understand what they mean.

Then they turn serious. They tell us tragic stories of how many concentration camp survivors died after their liberation because of the gifts of the Allies. One soldier starts to cry and tells us of his horror when they liberated a camp named Dachau a few weeks earlier. In front of them was a mountain of dead bodies and standing and sitting were living skeletons with huge sad, hollow eyes. My mind is barely able to register the shocking image he creates, and I instantly erase it, as I have learned to do so well.

The soldier says he gave a woman chocolate and she died soon after. The medics came and warned the soldiers, "Do not give out the chocolate or the cans of sardines and meat; not yet. If a starving person eats too much, too fast, they will die."

The soldier is such a young boy, he still has pimples on his face and he is sobbing with sadness and guilt over what he, in his kindness, has done. None of us can stand that irony: sudden death upon liberation because of the generosity of the liberators.

We save the chocolate for when we will feel happier and plan to trade the cigarettes for food. The last part of our journey becomes more difficult because the Americans are now strictly forbidden to pick us up, so we look for other trucks and we walk. We sleep at night in the fields, still frightened that the Algerian soldiers will find us. We try to keep ourselves clean by washing in the rivers. It feels like this trip will never end.

JUNE 1, 1945

At last we arrive in Munich. It has taken us three weeks. We go to look for Jews. We are told that there is a large group of survivors being sheltered in the Deutsches Museum in the center of Munich. We walk there and, yes, here we find Jews. Real Jews. And by joining their number we let drop the masks we've been hiding behind these last three years and re-inhabit our own Jewish faces.

Just like the American soldiers told us, some truly look like skeletons, with hollow, dead eyes, but some look like us, healthy and free, and some are as white as snow from hiding in attics and behind walls for five years. Surprisingly, there are many children, but their legs are like toothpicks. They can barely walk because they were hidden in barrels, in coffins, in sofas, in closets, between walls. Their young growing bodies never had exercise and never saw the sun. But now we are Jews, all together, and alive and safe. A few of the children just sit and stare at the ground, but most of them are running around like real children and we young Jews start to meet others our age and talk and talk and talk.

But we do not talk about the past. We flirt with one another and we talk about the dance tonight and the walk along the river and the picnic planned for tomorrow. We must look forward. We must never look back or we will go mad.

The American Hebrew Immigrant Aid Society, HIAS, is there at the museum and they are trying, with the Red Cross, to help all of us. They are writing down the names of the survivors and we stand in lines to put the names of our families on the List of the Missing, while we are on the List of the Found.

We need to register with the HIAS. They will give us real identity cards as displaced persons (DPs) under our real names and countries of origin. It will not have *Jew* stamped on it. Sabina has no doubts about who she is. Janina Sieracka is gone and she is again Sabina Markowitz. But with all I have learned about the devastating losses in this war, I feel as if Sura Gitla is dead. Gucia's innocent idealistic life is finished. There is no present or future for her. I had good luck and survived as Danuta Barbara Tanska. I feel strong and adult as Basia. And to be honest, Gucia identifies me as a Jew. I feel safer with Barbara, who could be anyone. I tell the HIAS woman that my name is Barbara Gomolinska and so it is. They give us our IDs and a little money. With that and what we had saved from our wages, Sabina and I can afford to rent a small room.

We answer an ad for a room with the Schwartzkopfs, a German family, and when we tell them we are Jews they say it is fine with them. They tell us they never liked Hitler and that they never knew about the concentration camps or the extermination of the Jews. Actually, they tell us, some of their best friends were Jews. We hear this same story from Germans over and over and over again. Nobody knew about the fate of the Jews and nobody supported Hitler. Of course we don't believe them but we certainly don't question them. For our own sanity, we must let it go for now. For the first time in five years Sabina and I can stand tall and feel safe. We are still young and we have the rest of our lives in front of us.

Piotrków

*My eyes shed streams of water over the
ruins of my poor people.*
—Lamentations 3:48

JULY 1945

I cannot wait any longer. I really must go home. I have been able to contact Janek to let him know I am alive and in Munich. He writes back that he is going to Piotrków and Idek and Josek are alive and already there and Uncle Josef, too. How I long to see them and to see what is left of Piotrków, even daring to hope of rebuilding our lives together there. Unbelievably, I have just learned that Hela and Marek survived the Bergen-Belsen Concentration Camp and are living in the DP camp there. And that is what is left of our large family.

Sabina cannot bear the thought of going back because she knows she has no one to go back to. Except for me, she is truly alone in the world. She gives me a letter for Leon Reichmann and tells me to give it to him when I see him. When I see him! She has no doubts that he is alive and that they will get married. She has no doubts about her mother's advice in her dream. I think the memory of that dream has kept Sabina going.

At the Deutsches Museum there are other Jews from Poland who want to go back, too, so we decide to all take the train together. If there is any doubt that Hitler is no longer running Germany, one need only look at the railway system. Once so precise and dependable, the trains stood as a shining example of the Führer's restoration of Germany to its rightful place of superiority to all other nations. Now the rail system is in total chaos. All we know is where a train is heading and where it will stop along the way. No one can predict when it will leave or how long it will be between one stop and the next.

When we get on the train we learn that it will stop in Ulm and stay there in the station for several hours. I do not question the powerful impulse that guides me to get off the train in Ulm. I tell my companions to wait for me.

I feel surprisingly calm knocking on the door, not sure who will answer. The Gasthaus zum Rotter Lowen has been repaired from the bomb blast. Herr Schweibold opens the door. His only show of feeling is the slight pause before he finds the words to welcome me in. I am disappointed to learn that his wife is not there. He is not a bad man, and like so many others, endured the war by taking care of himself, keeping his head down, and staying out of trouble. Frau Schweibold, however, was a true Nazi.

I remember so clearly, one time, when Sabina and I were peeling potatoes in the kitchen, Frau Schweibold was cursing the evil Allies for the devastating bombing they were inflicting on Germany. As she uttered one of her self-righteous, arrogant opinions, for once I decided not to play it safe and hold my tongue. "But Germany started it by bombing Poland!" I argued.

"Oh," she replied with a dismissive flick of her wrist, "those bombs were just meant for the Jews."

I felt so angry at her hatred and stupidity. Fortunately, I didn't say what I was thinking: that I never knew bombs could be anti-Semitic.

As we sit over coffee I tell Herr Schweibold why I have come. I want him and Frau Schweibold to know that Junka and I are Jewish. His expression remains placid.

"I thought maybe that was so," is all he says.

I don't believe him, but I see there is nothing more I can do. And there is really nothing more that I need. I came and said what I had to say. I'm only sorry I couldn't say it to his wife. I return to the station and tell my companions I was just walking around to see how everything looked since I had left. Now I am ready to look forward to where I am going, not back to where I've been.

Poland is now occupied by the Soviets so to get there we have to go through the Russian Zone, which we cannot legally do because we don't have the right papers. So we get off the train near the border, walk in the forest following the tracks, and stop in little villages in Czechoslovakia. We feel bold and exuberant as we enter the bars and cafés along the way, singing and dancing and laughing. We feel as if nothing bad can happen to us ever again. Then we walk across the border into Poland and get on the train at the next station.

The train stops at the familiar station in Piotrków. My heart is beating wildly, my stomach is cramping. I realize that it is exactly four years since my mama died. I walk to the address Janek sent, a part of a neighborhood I am not familiar with. I knock and the door opens and I see what is left of my family.

Idek and Josek and Janek and Uncle Josef hug me and kiss me and we cry with happiness and relief. I tell them what I have heard about Hela and Marek. But we say not a word about the past. We can't think or talk about the atrocities. We must try to forget our nightmares. We must try to move into our future.

Janek and I go for a walk. The lindens are in bloom and the smell is sweet. We find a bench in the Rynek Trybunalski. It is almost deserted, desolate. There are a few old Poles walking around, but there are no more Jews.

"Tante Sura?" I ask.

"The gentile who was hiding her was denounced by his neighbor and the whole family was turned in," he says. "Mama and the Polish family were all sent to Auschwitz."

I shiver.

"Tatte was luckier," he continues. "The brave gentile family who hid him was never turned in and so he is still with us."

"And Mendel and Sprintza and all the cousins?"

"Elkanah was at the glass factory until this January. He survived Buchenwald. All the rest are gone," he says, looking at his feet.

"But how did my brothers survive?" I whisper.

"Idek and Josek were together at the slave-labor camp at Bugaj until the Nazis closed it and put all the male workers on a train to Buchenwald," says Janek. "While changing trains, Josek made a run for it into the woods and walked to a farm where there was a Polish woman. Maybe she knew he was a Jew, maybe not. She said she needed someone to take care of her horse. Josek said that before the war he had spent his whole life working on a farm taking care of horses."

I laugh. For the first time since I have gotten to Piotrków, I can laugh. "The closest he ever came to a horse was the one in our stable, and he never looked at it!"

"Of course," Janek says with a smile. "Of course. So the next day, just Josek's luck, the horse died! But the woman kept him on the farm anyway, doing all the heavy work. Idek wasn't so lucky. He didn't want to risk trying to escape, so he ended up in the concentration camp in Buchenwald. But he is lucky enough that he is alive."

"And what do you know of Hela and Marek before the liquidation?"

"I know from Josek and Idek that Hela was protected by working with her brother-in-law, Abek, in the Nazi uniform shop, and then she, too, was sent to work at Bugaj. But a small child who couldn't work was worth nothing and would certainly have been killed. So each day when they went to work, Idek and Josek took six-year-old Marek with them, hidden in a sack slung over one or the other's back. Each evening they would bring him back to Hela at the barracks where they all slept. When they closed Bugaj, Hela and Marek were sent to Ravensbrück. It's amazing that Hela, much less Marek, survived."

I stay in Piotrków for a month, always carrying Sabina's letter to Leon Reichmann in my purse, but never seeing or hearing word of him.

One day, while Idek and Josek are out for a walk, I go to the house of Pani Zbeingska, the Polish woman who kept our remaining possessions and sent Regina back to die. When Pani opens the door, I demand she return what she stole from my family. She spits at me and screams *"Zhid!"* and slams the door in my face.

Shaken by memories of my red-haired younger sister and this woman's hatred, I rush to the apartment where we are staying and tell everyone what has just happened. Janek looks at us somber and upset. "Since I've been here, I've been hearing terrible rumors about the Poles stealing from and killing the returning Jewish survivors. Just an hour ago, I heard another sickening story," he says. "Do you remember Ben Helfgott?"

None of us do.

"I suppose he was too young for you to have known him. He's now fifteen. He and his twelve-year-old cousin miraculously survived Theresienstadt. Just after the Liberation, hoping to find some shred of family left, they tried to take the train to Piotrków but were stopped by two Polish policemen. They were taken to a totally deserted street with vacant buildings. The police took out their guns and told the boys to stand against the wall. Can you imagine, after all they had gone through, to come home to this? Ben started crying and begging for their lives. One of the policemen said to the other: 'Okay, they're just young boys.' And turning to Ben he said, 'But you are very lucky to be left alive. We have already killed many of your kind.'"

We are shaken and all sadly realize that Poland and Piotrków can no longer be a home for us. The loss, the memories, are too painful. And we see that the Jew hatred under the Polish Communists is even worse than the anti-Semitism we grew up with. Josek, Idek, and I decide to leave and go to the DP camp at Bergen-Belsen to stay with Hela.

On the day we leave, as I walk through Rynek Trybunalski, who should I see but Leon Reichmann! He looks like Gandhi, he is so skinny, but otherwise he looks well and I give him Sabina's letter. I tell him Sabina and I are living in Munich. He says to tell her he will come.

Hela and Marek

During five years from my childhood I was in the hell
of the camps, under the threat of death expected at any moment,
lacking information as to what would happen at
the next moment and I survived. I chose life.
The years of my childhood in the Holocaust left on me
an ineffaceable mark. I drew from my strength of
spirit resources which enabled me to cope and to win.
The Nazis could not defeat me.
My memories from the Holocaust as a small child
are a testimony to the resistance of the spirit against
inhumanity, horrors, cruelty and the baseness of spirit of
the Nazi Germans who saw themselves as cultural and
spiritual people enlightened above all.
—Marek (Moshe) Brem, written in Haifa, Israel, 2007

AUGUST 1945

My brothers and I take the train from Poland through Czechoslovakia to Bergen-Belsen, getting off before the border, dodging the Soviet border guards, going to cafés and even a few cabarets at night. Trusting the

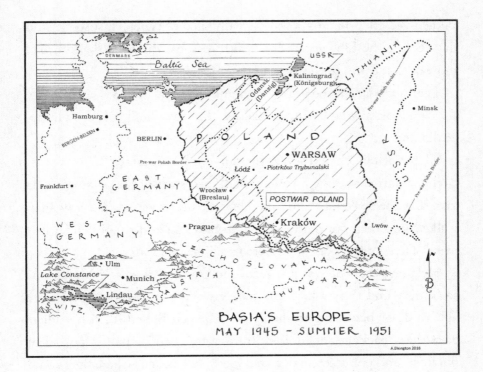

BASIA'S EUROPE
MAY 1945 – SUMMER 1951

A.Elkington 2016

German mail system more than the Polish, the minute the train stops in Germany I mail a letter to Sabina to tell her of the good news that I found Leon, gave him her letter, and that he said he would go to her.

The train arrives at Bergen-Belsen. I have no idea what I will find when we get off. Those first visions of the DP camp in Munich are seared in my brain. Will my older sister Hela look like those skeletons with dead, hollow eyes? Will my young nephew, Marek, have toothpicks for legs and the look of an old man?

But there they are! Laughing and smiling and waving at us, looking thinner, but almost like themselves. We hug and kiss and cry and cling to one another; the remnants of our once large, happy family of Piotrków.

We stay with Hela and Marek in their room in a former German military barracks just outside what had been the concentration camp of

Bergen-Belsen. So many Jews tragically died of typhus just weeks and days before the Liberation. For health reasons, the Allies had burned most of that camp to the ground.

I cannot stop staring at my sister and nephew.

"You look so wonderful, so healthy," I say as I hold Marek's plump, pink hand.

They both laugh and say, at the same time, "Potatoes!"

They start chattering together to tell their story of the potatoes. Hela says that the sweetest words she has ever heard were when a woman walked into their concentration camp barracks and simply said, "It is over." They knew at last they were free. They had survived.

Hela says that she was just recovering from typhus and Marek was so hungry and thirsty he could barely walk, but somehow they were able to drag themselves to the gates of Bergen-Belsen. British soldiers gave them packages of food, a knife, a fork, and a pan, a pound of potatoes, and pointed to a deserted German barracks where they could stay. Hela immediately found a water tap, peeled the potatoes, and in their safe little room cooked the potatoes in the small pot. Marek is excited and says they were so hungry they couldn't wait. He kept taking the potatoes out from the boiling water and eating them. His eyes light up and he tells me that the taste of those potatoes was the most wonderful taste of any food. He is sure that he will love simple warm boiled potatoes until he becomes an old man and I understand exactly what he is saying. I feel the same way about those glorious boiled potatoes and remember all the weight I gained in Ulm while I peeled potatoes and shared them with the pot.

Hela laughs again and says she has spent the months since the April 15 liberation of Bergen-Belsen peeling and cooking potatoes, and Marek and she still eat and eat because their stomachs cannot yet be filled up. Marek will not let her throw the boiled potato water away but drinks it with relish, like soup. Marek says the potatoes have ended the war for him, though not all its nightmares.

Marek takes my hand to go for a little walk. He says he cannot get enough of the blue sky and the sunshine and the freedom to just walk around. There are so few children for him to play with and he is the youngest by far. But he says he doesn't mind playing by himself. He has spent so many years hidden alone, in the dark, afraid to say a word, afraid he would be taken from Hela. And now in the daytime he feels so calm and free. Nighttime is another matter, and he shudders.

"Auntie Gucia, remember that terrible German soldier, Wilhelm, with his dog? After you left, Wilhelm let the dog into Zayde's house while we were eating supper, but Lulek and I ran to the armoire and crawled under it and the dog couldn't get us. And did Uncle Josek tell you about the big bag? Uncle Abek always knew when there would be an *Aktion*. It was so terrible, so many people were forced onto the trains. Uncle Abek would come at night and Mamashi would put on some of Papa's clothes with a big hat to hide her face and Uncle Josek would put me in a big bag with a little hole so I could breathe, and he would carry me on his shoulders. He told me we were playing the Quiet Game and if I made any sounds at all, I wouldn't win. We walked very far and stayed in the house of the Persinskis. Do you remember them? The nice Polish people who worked for my Zayde Brem? We had to stay in their dark basement for days until Uncle Abek would come to get us and tell us it was all right to come home. At night, when there was no moon, the Persinkis would let us go into the fields, but we had to keep playing the Quiet Game. It was such a relief to come home and be let out of the bag.

"That happened many, many times," he says, with a solemn look on his face.

I hug him again, remembering that cheery, pink-cheeked little boy with curly red hair. The curls are all gone and the cheeks are no longer plump and pink, but he still has his sweet, though now more grave, expression.

"Uncle Abek and Mama sewed for the Germans and Mama cooked for them, too. They loved her patés, onion rolls, and egg liquor. But when I was six, the Nazis took a lot of people to the Rakow Forest and shot them. Uncle Abek was one of them. Uncle Josek, Uncle Idek, and Mamashi were sent to the Bugaj Labor Camp to work at the carpentry factory. My job was to stay out of the way," he says.

We stop walking and his face clouds over. "It was all right until they closed the factory and we all had to go on the trains," Marek says quietly. "They made the men go away from the women and they tried to make me go with Uncle Josek. But Mama said that I would stay with her. She said what would be her fate would be my fate. She would not give me up and she held me tight," he says proudly.

We start to walk again.

"They told Mama to take off her boots and throw them in a big pile with all the others. But at the station we found Uncle Idek, and he was furious at Mama. Didn't she know that Zayde Brem had melted down all the family gold and put some of it in the heels of her boots? It was meant to save her and me! We ran back to the pile and searched and searched and, Auntie Gucia, I was only six, so I started playing with that great big pile of shoes. I threw them up as high as I could, and suddenly I found Mama's boots. Imagine that! She was so proud of me. She says over and over again that those boots and what was hidden in them saved us many times from death and hunger."

He speaks with fierce confidence like a little man, this usually quiet and modest child. What an incredible miracle he is.

"We were squeezed on a train for a long, long time. Mama let me climb on her shoulders so I could see out of a little window with bars.

We got out at a place called Ravensbrück. When the women guards told us to take off all our clothes and leave everything outside in a pile and then go to the showers, Mama hid a tiny bit of the gold from the boots and swallowed the rest. She gave the guard the gold coin and we were able to take a shower in a private room and get our own clothes back. I was really disgusted with how Mama got the rest of the gold back. You can imagine how, can't you, Auntie Gucia? And I was so very angry with Mama that she meekly allowed them to shave her head of its beautiful mane of strawberry-blond hair. Now that I am older, I understand what she had to do and I feel ashamed that I cried and raged at her for allowing herself to be so humiliated.

"I think it was late fall and the beginning of a cold and snowy winter. We were put in a long, dark, and cold hut, with wooden bunks three floors high, with pads, not mattresses. I was so lucky because I found a thin blanket and still had my own clothes.

"Every morning before sunrise we had to go outside for roll call. That was the worst part of the day for me. Every day I would grab both of Mama's legs and make her promise she would come back after her work and keep me from the Germans. Then Mama and all the women had to go to dig potatoes from the frozen earth and put them in large crates to be carried to a large building. They worked until dark and I had to stay hidden all day in the dark hut. The lice were my only playmates and I learned how to catch them very well," says Marek, smiling at his joke.

"Mama was able to buy tobacco with her gold. She met some Dutch girls in another part of the camp. They were allowed to receive food packages from Holland and Mama traded the tobacco for food for me and her.

"Just a few months ago, I remember it so clearly," Marek says as he looks up at the sky, "during one of the roll calls, I saw a plane flying very low. I could see the blond, mustached pilot with his leather hat. Then there was a large squadron of planes. Some of the women said they were American planes flying to Berlin. But even this could not give us hope, standing there in the freezing, dark cold. A few days later, we were all rushed onto trains to here, Bergen-Belsen. I remember while we were waiting for that train, I saw a full moon, shining in all its glory, and I thought that some parts of this world still had true beauty.

"When we got here, they took us down to huts where we were crammed together with Gypsies and their children. We Jews were on one side; the Gypsies on the other. This time there were no pads or blankets, just a hard floor on which we tried to sleep. Mama still had a little gold left but the German guards had nothing themselves, and so there was not a lot of food to exchange for Zayde Brem's gold.

"Auntie Gucia, that time was the worst of all." He shudders and we stop walking.

I sit on the ground and he sits on my lap. I hug him tightly and it feels delicious to have his small warm body close to mine. "The Gypsies just turned their faces to the walls and died. Most of the time there was no water to drink. We had to use the dirty, melted snow. So many people got terribly sick and died. One day the Germans brought a few buckets of real water. I was so thirsty that I couldn't stop crying and Mama rushed to get water for me. A German hit her so hard on her head she was bleeding. I felt so guilty. I promised myself I would never ask her for water again. Then Mama got so sick and hot, and all I could do was sit by her and kill the lice. And then the woman walked in and said, 'It's over.'"

And Marek gets off my lap and goes running through the fields with his hands outstretched, laughing at the sun and the sky.

I envy Marek. He still has his mother. She survived the typhus.

Remembering my own dear mama, I feel a deep, painful emptiness.

Whenever I think of her, and I often do, I cherish the deep intimacy of those last days of her life as I tried to make her well. It was a chance to repay a little bit of all the love and care she had given to me. And now, sitting with Hela and Marek in Bergen-Belsen, I think that perhaps Mama's death saved her from the later horrors of the emptying of the ghetto and the extermination camps that Tatte and Beniek and Regina had to experience. And I know that if Mama had been alive in 1942, I never would have fled the ghetto. I would have stayed with my family. I realize that Mama's death gave me life.

And though I would never wish otherwise, I now have my bossy older sister back. After a month in Bergen-Belsen, I realize I do not belong here. Hela, still the big sister, wants to take care of me and tell me what to do all the time. Even though we are both adults who have been through hell and survived, she still wants to tell me what to wear, what to eat, what to think, what to plan for my future. Like Marek, I look at the vast blue sky and realize I need some freedom. I take the train and go back to Munich and Sabina.

Munich

*The Jew saw them all, survived them all, and is now what
he always was, exhibiting no decadence, no infirmities of age,
no weakening of his parts, no slowing of his energies,
no dulling of his alert but aggressive mind. All things are
mortal but the Jews; all other forces pass, but he remains.
What is the secret of his immortality?*
—Mark Twain (1835–1910)

SEPTEMBER 1945–MARCH 1946

It's very late when I get off the train in Munich. It is a cold autumn
night and the trees, the few that are still standing after the bombing,
have lost all their leaves. I am eager to see Sabina, and I walk as quickly
as I can to our little room.

We hug and kiss. And she tells me that she has been desperately lonely.

I am so fortunate. I have two brothers, a sister, a nephew, an uncle,
and two cousins. She has no one in the world. Leon wrote to her in
August to say that he had gotten her letter and that he will come to
Munich. She is waiting for him, but it has already been a month.

And then she tells me the latest terrible news.

"Basia, I felt so alone without you, so I went to the DP camp at the Deutsches Museum. Everyone was talking about what had just happened in Kraków. Poles had been throwing stones at returning Jews, robbing and beating them. Then they accused some of the Jewish survivors of killing Christian children and hiding them in the Kupa Synagogue. A Polish mob ran into the synagogue, can you believe it, it was on Shabbos, and they beat the men who were praying there. They burned the Torah. Then they burned the synagogue. The Jews who were hurt were taken to the hospital, where a mob entered and beat the wounded again. Basia, I've heard that horrible things like this have been happening all over Poland."

I can't believe what I'm hearing. I want to cover my ears. It can't be true. Not after what we have all been through. Another pogrom, so soon?

We need to be with our people. To feel safe and secure. We spend the autumn and winter going to the Jewish Relief Center at the Deutsches Museum every day. We eat our meals there and visit with all the survivors. So many of them are young and full of such excitement to be alive. We sing and dance and flirt and do everything we can to keep busy. We cannot allow our minds to dwell on the past or our losses for even one second. Instead we are eager to begin building our futures. Now that we are no longer hungry for food, we feel a passion to devour life.

But still, for Sabina, no word from Leon.

Sabina is so disappointed. She realizes that if Leon really cared about her he would have come by now or at least sent word. I have been seeing a charming man whose passionate pursuit of me is quite flattering at first. But soon I get tired of his aggressive efforts to win me over, not respecting my wishes to hold him at arm's length. There are even rumors that he has a wife somewhere. I start to question his honesty.

To escape his pressure, I flee Munich and join Hela, Marek, Idek, and Josek back in Bergen-Belsen. But after a few weeks, Hela gets on my nerves again.

I decide it is time to go back to Munich.

The only way to travel between Bergen-Belsen and Munich is a car ride to Frankfurt and then by train to Munich. A few of the DPs at the camp dabble in the black market and they have cars, so whenever one of them is going to Frankfurt, he puts up a notice offering others a ride in exchange for sharing expenses.

When a notice appears I sign up and get a note back telling me what time to meet the next day. My driver is another survivor from Poland, and I am surprised that there are no other riders. Usually there are more people than can fit in one car.

After driving for about two hours, making meaningless chitchat along the way, he discovers that he is having "car trouble" and we can go no farther but must spend the night at a nearby inn. When we go to check in and the woman at the front desk asks if we want one room or two, he immediately answers, "One."

Can you imagine? Without a glance in my direction and not a moment's hesitation, "One." Car trouble, indeed.

What nerve! I look at the woman and immediately and emphatically say, "Two rooms!" And that's the end of that. We get two rooms. The next morning we drive off to Frankfurt. For the entire drive he speaks to me brusquely and only when necessary, which is quite fine with me. (It seems that whenever I look to a man for help or safety, it is a matter of luck whether he will in fact be my rescuer or another dangerous predator; whether Polish or German, Jewish or gentile. My only conclusion is that some men are like dogs.)

It's starting to get dark as I rush from the Munich train station to our room. I can't wait to tell Sabina what has happened. But I am shocked when I walk in. There is Abram Altus sitting with Sabina. I hug her and kiss her and notice that there is now a curtain hanging from the ceiling, separating her bed from mine. Sabina and I had met Abram at the DP camp some time before.

He was always quite attentive and eager to spend time with us, but neither of us was interested in more than casual small talk. Sabina and I had always found him a bit dull. He was far more religious than we and not a lot of fun. He told us that he was soon to immigrate to America and often boasted about his thriving business before the war. Yet he spoke in a rather uneducated way. We had met so many men at the Deutsches Museum who all had wonderful stories about their rich and successful pasts before the war. How could we know if they were telling the truth? But there is Abram sitting on Sabina's bed. And I understand her deep loneliness and her desperate need for someone to take care of her.

Abram must see that we want to be alone and talk, so he tells us that he is going out for a walk and a smoke. Right away I tell Sabina about the trip from Bergen-Belsen and the shocking gall of the driver pretending to have car trouble and then thinking he could share a room with me.

"He must have been so angry. He could have left you right there!" Sabina says, at first concerned. But then she smiles and says I should have used Rachel's ploy.

"Rachel?" I don't understand what she means.

"Basia, don't you remember the stories of all the marvelously clever women in the Torah? Remember, in Genesis, when Rachel stole her father's idols and hid them in a camel cushion? When her father came looking for his idols, she sat on the cushion and said, 'The time of woman is upon me,' meaning it was her time of the month when it was forbidden for any man to touch a woman." Sabina laughs.

Her laugh is such a beautiful sound; she has been sad for so long, she rarely laughs.

"So, tricked by his daughter, Laban no longer had his idols to worship. That idiot of a man tried to trick you, so you could have done the same. You should have said to him: 'I am unclean; the time of woman is upon me.'" She laughs again.

At first I'm not in a mood to think it is very funny. "What, so in two weeks he comes back? After telling everyone in Bergen-Belsen that I'm his girlfriend?" I say.

Then, instead of feeling outrage, I see the humor.

We both laugh and hug. "Sabina, thank you for the story," I say, "but you know I could have never said that to a man. He's lucky he didn't get a slap. He wanted my money so he didn't strand me and now I'm back here with you."

Again we hug. I am close to tears, feeling such relief from such a simple gift: to be with a true friend I know and trust.

Abram comes back smelling of cigarettes. It is late and Sabina closes the curtain. She is with Abram but I know that she is still thinking of Leon. Why has he not written or contacted her? And then, later that very evening, Frau Schwartzkopf runs to our door to say that there is a telephone call for Fräulein Markowitz. It's Leon. He has finally called.

Sabina comes back to the room, her face glowing. Leon is in prison in Frankfurt and he needs her to come get him out. She quickly packs a small overnight bag and is gone, leaving me alone with Abram Altus in our tiny room, a thin green cotton curtain between us. I feel very uncomfortable and cannot imagine spending even another night this way. If Sabina doesn't come home tomorrow, I will have to find another place to live.

Leon

My beloved spoke thus to me:
"Arise, my darling.
My fair one, come away!
For now the winter is past,
The rains are over and gone,
The blossoms have appeared in the land."
—Song of Solomon 2:10–12

MARCH–APRIL 1946

Fortunately for me, Sabina comes back the next morning, Leon Reichmann with her.

She tells me that she now understands that her dream of her mother was just that—a dream. If Leon wanted to be with her, he wouldn't have waited nine months to call her. And when she told him about her new relationship with Abram Altus he encouraged her. She understands that his caring for her is not romantic. Like her, Leon has lost everyone. He is left alone to build his new life without the comfort and support of family. Not only does Abram offer a family to become part of, but they live in Detroit, Michigan, and—once she and Abram marry—his brother will sponsor them to immigrate to America! She tells me she now sees that dreaming of Leon gave her something to live for during those last months of the war; but the life she is meant for is with Abram. So she is at peace and happy to see her old friend.

Leon looks so much better than when I saw him back in Piotrków. He's still skinny but looking more robust and wearing a beautiful soft black leather jacket and wonderfully tailored pants. Leon says that he was arrested by the Americans because he was trying to make some money, something about selling coins on the black market. Such a strange world. We Jews are almost exterminated by the Nazis while the whole world watches and does nothing. Then we are liberated but not given any help for our future. So many survivors were left on their own when the camp gates were opened. They had to find their way to their hometown or to a DP camp. They had no money and most had no food or shelter. And now that we finally find a way to do some business so that we can take care of ourselves, we are punished.

Leon has set up a thriving business in Frankfurt and Berlin, some of it legal, some not, selling watches, scrap metal, and other goods that he can buy in Poland and sell to the Germans, who can't cross the border. Now he is planning to do the same in Munich. He was able to get started with some gold and money that he and his mother had buried in their backyard soon after the ghetto was formed. When I met him in Piotrków, he had just dug up the money and was on his way to starting his business.

I feel so comfortable talking to someone from my hometown. I never knew Leon well, just that he was Jacob Brem's best friend and sometimes came to our house for their card games. But of course I knew of him: his fine family, their successful business, the gentle care he took of his mother after his brother was killed that first horrible week of the war.

But I feel a bit awkward. Leon and Sabina treat each other as friends, but he directs most of his attention to me. That very day he rents a room from Frau Schwartzkopf. Then he asks me to go out to dinner with him that night and brings me flowers when he arrives. I can't eat very much because I have a terrible toothache and he offers to pay for the cost of the dentist. He wants to buy me leather boots. He even offers me a puppy. A puppy! I thank him and tell him I am having a hard enough time taking care of myself, much less a dog, and that I cannot accept such lavish gifts.

Later that night, Sabina tells me that Leon complained to her that I did not like him because I refused his gifts, but she told him not to give up.

The next day Leon gives me a beautiful amber-colored hat with a green feather. He says the amber matches my eyes. We go walking along the river. He takes me to the dentist after the walk. He tells me that he is not interested in Sabina, and anyway, on the train from Frankfurt to Munich, she had told him about Abram.

I ask him why he came to Munich and he says, "Because you are here."

And then Leon asks me to marry him.

It all happens so fast. I tell Leon that I will think about it, and he feels rejected because I cannot answer immediately.

But after two days I say, "Yes."

When I accept Leon's proposal, I am not in love with him. I barely know him. I wonder, after what has happened to my world and my innocence, if I can ever really fall in love again. But I know Leon's roots. He comes from a good family. I can trust him. He is a known quantity. And he is strong. I am so weary of having to make all my decisions. I am so tired of standing on my own two feet. I feel secure with Leon and I know that he will take care of me and that good character is the true basis for love. I know my future won't be easy, but it will be safe.

APRIL 9, 1946

My brother Josek offers to pay for the wedding. So three weeks later, here I stand under the *chuppa*, the bridal canopy, at Bergen-Belsen with this dark, thin man whom I both know like a *landsman* and know not at all, surrounded by the little family we have left; no one for him, and my two brothers, my sister, and my nephew for me.

Soon after, Sabina and Abram marry, and within two months she is pregnant.

Having lost all of her own family, Sabina is glad to be gaining a new family. She is especially thrilled to be adding her own blood, a child of her own, and an end to all that sad loneliness.

Marriage

In thy face I see
The map of honour, truth and loyalty.
—William Shakespeare, *King Henry VI*, Part 2

April 1946–February 1947

From the start, Leon is successful in his import-export business, though a little black market is surely a part of it. We are squeezed into his room at Frau Schwartzkopf's, but we live a comfortable middle-class life. I spend my days shopping for food to be prepared by the maid we have hired to do the cooking, and stopping by the seamstress for fittings; in the evenings we go to the opera or out to nightclubs with his business partners and their wives.

One evening, at dinnertime Leon comes to get me. "We will celebrate tonight. Get your hat," he says. And we go to a very elegant restaurant.

Over dinner he tells me that the Americans have just discovered a Nazi officer living in the upper flat of a large two-family house at 166 Agnes Bernauer Strasse. They have arrested the Nazi and offered the apartment and all the furnishings to Leon.

The next day we move into this magnificent palace. For the first time in a long while I feel safe and protected and pampered. Still, it is hard for me to breathe freely. The air feels so heavy. I cannot forget that the Germans methodically, cruelly exterminated six million of my people throughout Europe. I can still hear those words from the national anthem, *"Deutschland über alles,"* Germany, above all. So my delight in our beautiful new home is tempered by my discomfort over still living in Germany.

I tell Leon I can feel a band across my chest at the thought of staying here, but I also know we can't go back to Poland.

He nods and looks at me. Softly he says, "Basia, I just heard some terrible news from Poland. In Kielce, over forty Jews were killed because a Polish boy who ran away from his parents for two days claimed he had been kidnapped by Jews who wanted to kill him for his blood. You are right, Basia, we can never go back."

I feel sick and empty. Leon is right, we can never go back to Poland, and we certainly cannot stay in Germany. But where can we go? Will anywhere ever feel like home?

By now Hela has learned that Jacob survived the war and is alive in Israel, and she and Marek have left to join him. My friend Rozia also survived and has immigrated to Eretz Yisrael, where she was reunited with Sala. But all of them, as much as they would welcome us back into their lives, warn us of the many hardships of life in Israel. Conditions are austere because of all the shortages and the difficulty in earning a living. And of course there is the unpredictable, sporadic violence with the British and sometimes the Arabs.

Leon and I had been ardent Zionists, although at opposite poles politically—he on the right, I on the left. Before the war we would never have considered marrying. Now those differences seem less important.

Despite all those years when we each dreamed of living in Israel, now we both come to the heartbreaking decision that this is not to be. Leon and I know we cannot return to a life of fear and suffering and struggle. America, most survivors' first choice, requires a sponsor, someone with the means to ensure our financial support, and we have no one. Leon's cousin Meyer Reichmann, a prosperous attorney living with his wife, Luba, in Buenos Aires, Argentina, has offered to sponsor us there. I begin taking Spanish lessons.

The first night we spend in our new home, Leon and I finally talk about how we escaped extermination. It is such a painful subject that neither of us has wanted to talk very much about the past. Leon tells me that in October of 1941, at the same time that Josek and Idek were sent to the labor camp in Bugaj, he was sent to the labor camp at the Hortensja Glass Factory with his cousin Henry Marton. They were in the same workplace as my cousin Elkanah Libeskind, Mendel and Sprintza's son, and my neighbors, the rabbi's sons Tulek and Lulek.

"We were slaves. It was hell on earth," he says. "We endured backbreaking labor shoveling coal from the railroad cars and breathing in the fire of the ovens that made the molten glass. And we were the lucky ones!"

Looking back, Leon says, it saved their lives because they became "essential workers." They escaped the liquidation of October 14, 1943, when all of the rest of their families were shipped off to their deaths in Treblinka.

He tells me they all tried to help one another in the camp whenever they could. Early on, by offering a hefty bribe to a Nazi guard, Leon was allowed to sneak away a few times to his old home and dig up some of the money he had buried in his backyard. He used some of that money to buy extra food for Yisrael Lau, our Lulek—who was just a young child and was starving to death. His brother Naphtali (Tulek) was hiding him like Marek had been hidden. Later, when Naphtali was too weak to walk, Leon, himself also just skin and bones, carried Tulek on his back.

I was so proud of Leon when he told me this. What character he showed, that even when he himself barely had the strength or resources to survive, he would extend himself to help others in the camp. Hearing this story I know all over again that I have made the right decision to marry him. Not only is Leon strong, but he is clever and brave. It strikes me that Leon's role in the lives of these two boys mirrors their mother's role in mine; and as though in marrying him, fate has given me a way to thank her.

At one point, Leon didn't remember exactly when, the Nazis separated the workers and said they needed only those trained in certain trades: locksmiths, carpenters, shoemakers. Leon had worked in the wholesale construction business with his mother for years and had never done any specialized labor like that. The Nazis ordered the Jews with those skills to identify themselves. His cousin Henry, who was trained as a locksmith, raised his hand and nudged Leon to do the same, which he did. It was one of those snap decisions we all faced so many times during the war when your life is at stake and you don't know the outcome of going one way or the other. When the Nazis then brought each of the volunteers into a room to be tested, Leon feared he had just "volunteered" to get shot for lying. He saved his life by waiting for a moment when the guard wasn't looking and then running to join the men who had already passed the test and were lined up several yards away.

After the camp at Hortensja was liquidated in November 1944, he and Henry and all the other workers were put on trains to the labor camps at Czestochowa. In the commotion of getting off the train, Henry and Leon were able to run away to the house of a Pole Henry knew. They jumped over the wall and the Pole gave them blue Polish workers' uniforms and they were able to hide until the Liberation of 1945.

Only later is Leon able to tell me the most painful part of his story. In the early days of the ghetto he had married Sala Jacobowitz, who soon became pregnant. When her time came, they decided she would be safer passing as a gentile and going to the Polish hospital in town to deliver. But someone denounced her as a Jew. The day after she gave birth to a baby girl, they were both taken out and shot. Leon was never able to say goodbye to his wife. He never saw his little daughter.

New Lives

To everything there is a season,
and a time to every purpose under heaven:
A time to be born, and a time to die;
a time to sow, and a time to reap;
A time to kill, and a time to heal;
a time to break down, and a time to build up;
A time to weep, and a time to laugh; a time to mourn,
and a time to dance.
—Ecclesiastes 3:1–4

FEBRUARY 1947

I have just learned I am pregnant. If I could, I would keep this baby inside me forever; always within me and always safe. How I hope this child can heal some of Leon's pain over the baby he lost. We decide to delay our move to Argentina, not wanting to risk such a long ocean voyage with me in my condition.

And then we learn that Sabina has gone into labor. We visit her in the hospital after she delivers a baby boy. She and Abram are ecstatic and relieved that the baby is healthy. They name him Joel.

But why does Sabina have such a high fever? The doctor says that she has a raging infection. There are still many shortages even now, two years after the war, and the hospital has no antibiotics to treat her. The only hope is a blood transfusion, and Leon is the right blood type. That we could lose her now would be too cruel a joke.

But fate plays by its own rules, and four days later, after all we have been through, after we have survived this war together, after Leon has given his blood, Sabina is dead.

I have had my best friend, as close as a sister, torn from me. I cannot bear this. Will loss and grieving never end?

Soon Abram moves with the baby to Detroit. Not only will Joel never know his mother, he will grow up with only Abram to tell him about her. And Abram himself barely knew her.

SEPTEMBER 1947

But soon I am reminded that life offers gifts as well. I go into labor and Leon insists we go to Schwabing Hospital, more expensive and not as near but more established and more well-equipped than the local hospital where Sabina delivered. Though they have the most critical life-saving drugs, there is no anesthesia for childbirth and I suffer for many hours. But it is September 13, and while the war has shaken my faith in God, I am still, as my mother was, superstitious, and I am determined not to tempt fate by giving birth on the 13th. So somehow I hold on and at one a.m. on September 14, at the very start of the New Year, Rosh Hashanah, our precious daughter Helen—Hendla—is born.

Endings

Weeping may endure for a night
But joy cometh in the morning.
—Psalms 30:5

1947–1951

We bring Helen home from the hospital and soon after receive the extraordinary good news that we have been chosen by HIAS for sponsorship to immigrate to America. The Jewish community in Kansas City, Kansas, has offered to sponsor a small number of Jewish immigrants to come to America and by luck we are selected! It turns out to be four years before all the arrangements can be made. Those are happy years of watching our baby grow, taking holiday trips to Garmisch-Partenkirchen, saving a little money, and eagerly anticipating what lies ahead.

What a shock, then, to finally board our ship and endure two weeks of utter misery, crammed into steerage like human cargo. Thankfully, Leon is not affected by seasickness, so he can take care of Helen.

In Munich I had always been so dependent on our baby nurse, Leah, to help take care of Helen and I am already worried over whether I will know what to do. Now I am so sick the entire time, much worse than being pregnant, though not as bad as Liberation day, when I drank that entire bottle of vermouth.

Then we learn that because of a disastrous flood in Kansas City, the Jewish community there is no longer prepared to accept us, but the one in New Orleans, Louisiana, comes to our rescue. So even though a last-minute change of plans takes us by surprise, I am relieved that a new destination will shorten our voyage and that we will reach land in two days.

I am so grateful to leave that awful ship, feeling, not for the first time, the relief of escape. It helps, of course, that I can speak English. Poor Leon and Helen are lost in the strange noisy gibberish all around us. We feel a bit helpless and overwhelmed, but the kind woman from the New Orleans Jewish community who is there to meet us immediately takes charge and makes us feel welcome in our new home.

With my feet on the soil of America, for the first time in so many, many years, that tight band across my chest breaks. It is more than a sense of security for our future. The very air feels free. I feel as if my body has stretched wide open and at last I have all the room I need to deeply and fully breathe.

New Beginnings

AN AFTERWORD BY
HELEN REICHMANN WEST

For my mother, emigrating from Germany to start a new life meant that for the first time in twelve years she had a future. And for that future to be in America was a dream come true. America, a strong country safe from oppression, a country where all people lived with the universal human rights of freedom, security, equality, and justice.

1951: NEW ORLEANS

Though I was only four, I remember my feelings during our transatlantic crossing, which I must have absorbed from my parents: exhilaration; excitement; we're going to America! What had sustained my mother throughout the war was her belief that eventually America would enter and save the world. All she had to do was survive until then.

Yet alongside the thrill and confidence about what lay ahead in our new home, I know we felt a humbling vulnerability about being outsiders and alone. I had met a little girl on the boat to play with and I remember her talking excitedly about an uncle who would be there to greet her family when they arrived. How lucky she was, I remember thinking, that they would know someone. We were "newcomers," late arrivals where everyone else was well established, while we would be unfamiliar with, and to, everyone we met.

I came to learn that to take on the status of immigrant is a profound transformation that becomes part of who a person is: not just occasional moments of cultural awkwardness, but an ever-present lens through which one looks inward as well as out.

Arriving in America and finally feeling safe and free, my mother was caught off guard on her first shopping trip in New Orleans. She set her purse on a counter at a department store so she could hold on to me with one hand and have the other hand free to check out housewares for our new apartment. She wasn't being careless. She thought there was nothing to worry about, because in America everyone had what they needed, so of course no one would steal.

You won't be amazed, as she was, that when she returned to retrieve her purse, it was gone. This wasn't just the end of her purse. It happens. She'd survived much worse. This was the first unraveling of her deepest conviction: that the miseries people inflicted on each other would disappear if only they lived in a society free of poverty and dedicated to justice and equal rights. There would no longer be any reason for the worst traits of human nature. Greed, envy, violence—gone. And America, she believed, came as close as anywhere in the world to being that place. This was a future worth living for. It was a vision of humanity that got her through the most devastating explosion of inhumanity the world had ever seen. So this theft robbed her of a lot more than just her purse.

I'm touched by her idealism and naïveté after all she had lived through. It strikes me that the war years had interrupted the normal course of her development as a young person on the threshold of adulthood.

What there was to learn about life and human relations during the war was an aberration. Only now, at thirty-five, could she resume where she had left off at twenty-one.

My mother was soon in for another shocking disappointment when she got on a bus in New Orleans. She climbed aboard for her first outing and walked toward the back to take a seat. At first she couldn't make sense of what the driver was telling her. Then she realized from his gestures that he wanted her to move up front. She did but had no idea why. The bus drove along making stops and filling up; and then finally she understood.

All the black passengers went to the back, and when the seats ran out they stood crammed in the aisle. This was even though many of the seats in front were empty. In Poland she had had to sit in the back of her classes at university just because she was a Jew. Coming to America meant no one could make her sit in the back. That "honor," she now learned, was reserved for the blacks. This was how she learned about racial segregation. She told me it was ironic that she still couldn't sit where she wanted.

My father had gotten a job at a store that sold radios and some of the first television sets. His English wasn't good enough for him to be much help with the customers, but he was great at organizing and arranging stock and, with his skill with numbers and neat European hand, at keeping the books and accounts. The other employee was a black man who had been working there for thirteen years. The boss decided he needed a manager and promoted my father. It sickened my father that he should have any role in denying this other man what by rights of seniority and ability should have been his. He brought him home for dinner. Though it wasn't much, there was nothing else he knew to do. The boss fired my father for it.

We lasted in New Orleans for six months. My parents hated the racism. They had little in common with the Southern American Jews there. As kind and helpful as they were, my mother could only speak haltingly with them, and my father not at all. They couldn't tolerate the weather, found the culture as alien as the moon and, according to my mother, you couldn't find a decent loaf of bread. New Orleans would never feel like home.

Even though it meant giving up the financial support from the New Orleans Jewish community and depleting our paltry savings, my parents decided we'd move up north, where many Holocaust survivors had settled; the communities there might feel more European Jewish. My mother told me how low she felt leaving New Orleans. She was so weary of wandering. She had thought she was finally done with that, and here she was on another train looking for a place to live. She had to hold back tears as she rode past the backyards of houses where laundry hanging on clotheslines fluttered in the breeze. Everyone else has a place, she thought. Will there ever be a home for us?

1952–1957: BALTIMORE, MARYLAND

It had been thirteen years since my mother felt rooted and knew what "normal" felt like. What she got when we settled down in Baltimore was a far cry from anything she had imagined growing up in Poland or newly liberated in Germany.

My parents bought a grocery store, with living quarters attached, on a corner in a poor, mostly black section of East Baltimore. The living room and kitchen were behind the store and the two bedrooms, a small storage room, and a bathroom were upstairs. It was a neighborhood of broken-down old houses. There were housing projects across the street, three-story apartment buildings built in a square around a concrete inner courtyard where neighbors could visit and children could play, and this was where the smaller number of white people lived.

In those days neighborhoods like this were called slums. The term *ghetto* hadn't yet been appropriated for its current usage, but still retained the original meaning my parents knew all too well. We were the only Jews. We struggled with English and were just as foreign to our neighbors as they were to us.

The idea was that for five years my father and mother would work like dogs, live frugally while accumulating some savings and building up the business, and then sell the store for a nice profit. After that we would move up to a better business and a more comfortable life. Saving money was made easier by the backbreaking hours, which left my parents little time to spend anything. They worked from six in the morning till nine at night every day but Sunday, when they closed at two. The only time my father closed the store was for two days during the High Holidays. Some of our customers told my father they respected him for that. Eventually we adjusted, but the early days were especially hard.

Here's an idea of what we were up against. We'd been living in Baltimore for just a couple of months when one fall evening, after the store was closed, my parents and I were in our living room in back. Suddenly we heard a loud banging on the door and men yelling something we couldn't understand. Warily, my father opened the door to face three black teenagers wearing masks, demanding we give them candy.

We had never heard of Halloween. All we knew was that these wild men in disguise, yelling in English we had trouble making sense of, were demanding we hand over our stock-in-trade. We thought we were being robbed, and I was terrified. Seeing our confusion, the trick-or-treaters somehow managed to explain this ritual. Everyone relaxed, candy was disbursed, and we were relieved that rather than being held up, we'd just been initiated into a strange American cultural practice.

Before we got here, my family's common language was German, but now that we were in America, English was what we spoke at home. My parents spoke Polish to each other when they were alone or if they didn't want me to know what they were talking about. Eventually they made friends with other Holocaust survivors, mostly grocery-store owners like us, and the families would visit with each other on Sunday evenings. When we children were in the room everyone spoke English. The point was for the children to assimilate. But when we were off playing, the grownups spoke Polish or Yiddish. I managed to learn neither language. The only times this bothered me was when I was forced to sit through a boring evening at the Yiddish theater and didn't understand a word. It was especially frustrating when everyone laughed and I got ignored every time I asked what was funny. I understand now these were the dirty parts, the same as in Hebrew school when we would skip certain portions in our Torah study and I never knew why. So my parents kept one foot in their old world and one in the new. I don't think America ever really felt like home to them. As an immigrant, I, too, grew up feeling outside the mainstream culture and I became a psychologist because I wanted to know what "regular" people were like.

Over time my parents established themselves as important members of the community. The store was tiny, yet my father crammed the shelves with everything a family would need, all neatly and attractively arranged. I didn't much care for the huge glass jar of pickled pigs' feet next to the dill pickles and pickled onions, but other jars lined up by the cash register were filled with every penny candy a child might desire. Within easy reach on the shelves below were cookies and packaged pastries, the finest Hostess and TastyKake had to offer. And I could freely help myself, without asking, to as much as I wanted whenever I wanted.

Our store was a meeting place where people would regularly run into their neighbors and take a few moments to visit. One of the neighborhood teenage girls used to perch herself on top of the meat case and regale us and anyone else who cared to listen with the latest news about her social life and boyfriends.

My mother found herself in the very position she had spent all her years growing up in Poland working to avoid. She was determined to choose her life and not have it dictated to her, yet here she was stuck on her feet all day selling groceries. Raising me was her primary source of satisfaction. There wasn't much joy for her in those early Baltimore years, and I was the light of her life; her consolation prize, you might say.

She was an extraordinary mother, my greatest gift. I once commented to my husband that when I was a child, I believed that of all my friends I had the best mother, and he said, "I think you did." (Even today many of my friends use her as a role model for dealing with their own children, asking themselves, "What would Barbara do?") We had a relationship of total honesty and trust from the beginning—although a critical family event a few years later made clear that this wasn't an absolute truth.

There's a particular kind of impossible burden familiar to children of Holocaust survivors—to somehow make up for their parents' pain, certainly not add to it; to compensate for the missing years and opportunities, the lost futures and dreams. I've seen this play out in some mix of two ways. In some families, a child might grow up feeling guilty and dutiful and behaving in an obedient or rebellious manner, depending on his or her nature. For others, the pressure was to be happy. A challenging and complicated business in either case, but I prefer the second and that's what I had.

My mother and I were very close. As a young child I understood that I could never lie to her because she could read my mind. But the fact is I confided in her with full trust and she never betrayed that trust. Certainly I felt loved and cherished, and I can say that never, even during the infrequent moments of anger, was she ever once unkind to me. But what I now understand is rare, though I took it for granted at the time, was the respect she showed me from the day I was born. She regarded me as, and so I felt, equally a part of her and a separate autonomous being with dignity and rights. She never talked about my personal affairs with her friends because that would have been a violation of my privacy.

Not surprisingly, she raised me to think for myself and make my own decisions. The only restrictions she placed on me were those necessary for my safety and health. She was absolute about bedtime, no exceptions ever, no matter how annoyingly I pleaded every night for another five minutes. Not even once a year to watch *Peter Pan* on television. I was the only child in my class who couldn't watch it through to the end.

Eating was the other area over which we struggled. She was concerned that I was too skinny and was always trying to fatten me up, hence my total freedom at the candy and pastry counter in the store. Otherwise she took care in providing us with healthful and tasty meals, having improbably become quite an excellent cook. It was clear how deeply my parents cherished family, and so I loved all my relatives, most of whom I'd never met. These included the dead ones, most especially my grandmother and namesake, Hendla. This provided my mother with the most powerful weapon in her arsenal to get me to eat: "One more bite for Uncle Idek. One more bite for Cousin Marek. One more bite for Tante Sarka. One more bite for Tante Hela."

To me, this was not a game but serious business. I struggled to force myself to eat, believing that to refuse this food constituted rejection of the designated family member. (At that time, I hadn't even yet met my Tante Hela, who lived in Israel. Years later I came to appreciate the irony in eating for her when I learned that as a teenager, Hela would squirrel away leftover food from the rest of the family for herself and her friends.)

But other than that, I could do pretty much what I wanted and avoid what I didn't want to do. Within reason. And I was a reasonable child. The way my mother saw it, life says no often enough to build character. She loved me, so of course she would wish for me what I wished for myself, provided there was no harm or disrespect to others. Her philosophy was that a child's job was school, and done right that was a demanding job. Beyond that, children should be left free to enjoy childhood. Plenty of time later for chores and household responsibilities. It was up to me how and with whom to spend my time. Whenever I complained of being bored and whined, "Mommy, what should I do?" I never got an answer other than "I don't know. What do you want to do?" She treated me as someone reliable, trustworthy, and capable of understanding at her level, and so I was. She cared what I thought. I recommend this as a child-rearing strategy.

The only thing missing was a sibling. I desperately wanted a brother or sister to love and to play with. I also wanted a puppy, as did my father. But my mother refused, explaining you become attached to a pet, and then feel heartbroken when it dies. We know where that came from. Plus she knew she'd be stuck taking care of it.

So when I was eight and learned that she was pregnant, I was overjoyed. Henry was born on October 3, 1956. My mother was forty. He was a beautiful, affectionate baby and we all adored him. A year later my father sold the store, bought our first car, and moved us to Washington, DC. He bought a liquor store, in partnership with another Holocaust survivor, working only half the hours while making a better living. And instead of working every day as she had in the grocery, my mother now went in to help my father only on Friday or Saturday evening, whichever shift he worked that week. So life did become easier.

1960: Washington, DC

Two years after we moved to Washington the bottom fell out. I was twelve, Henry was three, and I was told that since Henry was born they had been hiding from me the devastating truth that he had Down syndrome. I didn't know exactly what that meant but I knew it was very, very bad. It was a moment of pure, inconceivable heartbreak. My mother and I were sobbing. This was one of the few times in her life, ever since her humiliation in first grade, that she wasn't able to control her tears. What finally forced the issue was the need to prepare me for what was coming. They were incapable of raising Henry without help and in those days that meant moving him to a residential facility.

When Henry was born my father had grieved and eventually coped. My mother had collapsed. She remained functional and responsible, but her spirit was extinguished and she sank into a depression on the order of her reaction to her mother's death from typhus. It certainly couldn't help her heal that for three years, in her efforts to hide all this from me, she had to try to act normal when she felt dead inside. Somehow she thought she could spare me, only nine years old, the pain of this hardship at such a young age. Better to wait until I was older, she thought, as though she could protect me from reality.

Years later, she told me that during that time, any kind of joy in life was beyond her imagining. It made no sense to her when people around her laughed.

One year later, when Henry was four, he was taken to live at the Forest Haven Children's Center in Laurel, Maryland, forty-five minutes away. Try to imagine strangers coming into your home and taking away your cherished, loving, uncomprehending toddler. The pain for all of us was more than I thought it possible to withstand. After all they had been through, I don't know how my parents ever got up off the floor. This was a blow to our family worse than a death, and most of all for my mother.

Eventually Henry adjusted to his new life and we adjusted to life without him. We spent each Sunday visiting with him in the parklike setting of his new home, and gradually our world again seemed "normal."

For my mother, the key to this was the introduction arranged by our pediatrician to two other couples with children in the same facility. Joining us on our Sunday visits were Lee and Rubin Obarzanek, also Holocaust survivors, and Herman and Frances Finkel. Frances was the real savior here. She was a latter-day Sprintza, standing four feet ten inches, with a huge personality, a little spark plug. She had a great sense of humor and even my mother, who hadn't laughed in years, couldn't resist cracking up. Frances and Herman were my parents' closest friends for the rest of their lives. They were like an aunt and uncle to Henry and me. My mother gradually came back to life.

1960–1978: Marriage

My mother had rightly recognized my father as a strong man who would take care of her. He was outgoing, energetic, responsible, reliable, and had a gift for business. He was also a sharp dresser and a great dancer. My father was the more adventurous of the two and always had to work to get my mother to agree to any break in their routine, like taking a vacation. She always loved these new adventures after the fact, and remained just as reluctant the next time he proposed one. He would try any new food. My mother, not.

"Basia, try this, it's delicious!"

"No, I don't like it."

"But how do you know if you never tasted it?"

"No, I don't want to."

"Please, just one bite!"

"No."

The occasions when my father got my mother to give in on this kind of thing were never.

My father was generous, both with money and time, and he was driven and proud. Because he grew up without a father, having lost his when he was just three, he had to figure out on his own what it meant to be a man. Success meant providing well, as he defined it, for his family, for which we would appreciate and respect him and the world would admire him. It hurt him that my mother refused a lot of his intended gifts. She wouldn't be caught dead in a mink coat, and she got him to compromise on an Oldsmobile instead of a Cadillac. Showy status symbols weren't for her, but he took it personally. It was no different than the leather boots and the puppy she turned down when he courted her in Munich, and why he complained to Sabina that my mother must not like him. So when my mother or I did ask for something, he was always glad to provide. He got as much from the giving as we got in the getting.

My parents didn't have the intellectual connection—my father had left school after eighth grade to help his mother run the family business—nor the easy compatibility she'd had with Heniek. But they did have the passion that she and Heniek were lacking. And like Heniek, my father made her laugh.

As independent and self-reliant as she'd always been, she also yearned to be looked after and taken care of. This was so even before the war, and especially after. She wanted a strong country to feel safe in and a strong husband to depend on, and she got both. Theirs was a traditional European division of labor. She was in charge of the household and children. My father ran everything else. He was a decisive, alpha kind of man who provided for his family, handled all the finances, and through wise investments left her well-off. You could rely on his word like a law of nature; if he said he would do something, it happened. My mother had never learned to drive so my father did all the driving, which also meant all the grocery shopping and getting me wherever I couldn't get myself on the bus.

Inevitably, a marriage between two strong personalities, one naturally geared to taking control and one unwilling to be bossed around, will have its deadlocks. Being ordered around by my father in the grocery store, getting criticized for how she wrapped a piece of fatback, wasn't the ideal arrangement for promoting marital harmony. This was what my mother hated most about those five years in the grocery store. At least in Washington she worked in the liquor store with him only one evening a week. Remember, this was a woman who realized she could never live on a *kibbutz* because she couldn't stand having other people tell her what to do.

My father was impatient and my mother was stubborn. He would escalate, she would resist. After his eruption, he would stop speaking and she would wait. She'd cook his meals and he wouldn't eat them. Eventually the cold war would blow over; it was never clear to me how.

Until one morning when I was about twelve, after a particularly nerve-racking few days of silent tension between them, when my father had been sleeping on the couch "because Daddy has a cold," I woke up to find them standing together in their bedroom, all smiles, a look of sweet contentment on my mother's face. So I guess that's how they made up.

It used to bother me that she wouldn't fight back when he lost his temper, would let him get away with it. But she insisted that would only make things worse. Some years after my father's death my mother told me the following story: She and my father were driving home from a vacation in the Catskills. Feeling particularly close and sentimental, he said to her, "You know, we're very lucky and we should be grateful for these thirty years that we've had together." "Yes," she said, "but if you count all the times you weren't speaking to me, it's really more like twenty." She said that from then on he never again gave her the silent treatment when she angered him. But what tickles me most about this story was her takeaway, which she told me in that droll, matter-of-fact way of hers: "I should have spoken up sooner."

1978: AFTER LEON

My father died of a heart attack on August 4, 1978. He was sixty-seven and my mother was sixty-two. Now that she was on her own, my mother had to face her insecurities and learn to do for herself everything my father used to handle. Nothing was more challenging than learning to drive. My mother was a physically unadventurous person. Growing up she had never learned to ride a bicycle, and after an accident while riding with Heniek on the handlebars of his bike, she never would. My mother carried herself with poise and grace, but underneath her refined demeanor she never lost the heightened anxiety that was her legacy from the war. This susceptibility to nervousness was transformed from the occasional startle reaction into an abiding part of her personality by a trauma having nothing to do with the war.

We were still living in Munich when she got news that her brother Josek had been struck by a car near Frankfurt and lay in the hospital unconscious. He had suffered brain damage, making it unlikely he would ever be the same, if he were to live at all. My mother left me with my father and Leah and rushed to his bedside. She and Hela and Idek took turns staying with him for weeks at a time over the three months that Josek lay in a coma. Once he woke up it took many more months of rehabilitation and healing to determine that there was no permanent damage to his physical functioning. Sadly this was not the case with his personality. Josek was never again the dynamic, clever, outgoing, and ambitious young man that he had been. I once asked my mother if she felt the war had changed her. She had survived the war and Sabina's death the same person she had always been, but it was this event, she told me, that coalesced all of it into an ever-present, moment-to-moment sense of the precariousness of life always hovering just under the surface.

Now, with my father gone, my mother faced a forced choice between two equal impossibilities: the abhorrent prospect of being dependent on anyone, including me, or facing her terror. She had always been resourceful about getting around on public transportation. (There had been two failed attempts many years earlier, when my father was determined to teach her to drive. Each campaign ended after one day, when they came home not speaking.) The one place she couldn't get to on her own was Henry's facility in Laurel, Maryland. Even though Herman or I drove her each Sunday, and were happy to do it, she wasn't willing to "impose" on anyone. So at the age of sixty-five my mother learned to drive. She signed up with an instructor, took lessons every day for three weeks, got her license on the first try, and became a competent and confident driver.

It's hard to reconcile my mother's basically cautious, risk-averse nature with the brave and dangerous chances she took during the war. My mother often said that she couldn't quite believe it herself. It was as though that were some other person, she used to say. But she also said, "When I'm in danger, I'm not shy."

One Friday evening before my father's death, when she was working in the liquor store, my parents were held up by two men with guns. As the robbers were leaving, having already emptied the cash register, one of them noticed the display case of Timex watches on the counter and grabbed a handful. "Haven't you taken enough?" she blurted. "Shut up, lady," he snapped, "or I'll blow your f**king head off." She was as affronted by the language as by the gun. I never heard a curse word come out of her mouth. The closest she came to foul language was exclaiming, *"Uh cholera!"*—the Polish equivalent of "Damn it!"—when she burned her finger on the stove.

It took five years for my mother to adjust to losing my father and for life to once again feel normal.

1993: Sabina's Son

Fifteen years after my father's passing, having failed in several previous attempts to locate Sabina's now-grown son, I tracked down his phone number in Seattle, Washington. I called, Joel answered, and I said, "My name is Helen West. Your mother and my mother survived the war together. Your mother and my father dated as teenagers before the war." After a few moments of silence while he absorbed what he'd just heard, he said that he was in the midst of putting his two young children to bed—the younger was a three-year-old girl named Sabina—and he would call back in half an hour.

We spoke for about an hour. I told him that my father had died of a heart attack at age sixty-seven, and that my mother and I had wanted to find him for some time, because we imagined he hadn't met many people who had known his mother. In fact, he said, we were the first. His father, also deceased, had been his sole source of information. His father had only known Sabina for barely a year, and his portrayal of her to Joel was filtered through his chronic depression. I told him what I knew about his mother. It was quite a different picture.

Following our conversation, Joel called my mother and they, too, spoke for about an hour. I sent him copies of photos we had of Sabina: one of her, my mother, and several young men posing playfully in front of the Deutsches Museum in Munich just after the war and another of Sabina in the countryside standing next to a horse and looking healthy and happy. There was also a picture of him as a newborn, with his mother's handwriting on the back, which she'd sent to my parents from the hospital.

Our last contact was a letter from Joel thanking us for troubling so to find him and for providing the missing pieces. There was so much about his mother he hadn't known, including the fact that she'd been married before. But what was most profound, he said, was gaining a sense of her not just as the lamented saint his father had described, but also as a real, live, flesh-and-blood human being who'd laughed and loved and actually lived.

2007: ONE MORE BITE

Until a month before her death, my mother and I brought Henry lunch every Sunday at his group home. By that time he was fifty-one, I was fifty-nine, and my mother was ninety-one. He still felt like our baby.

Like many people with Down syndrome, Henry was born with a heart defect, so each time she brought him the same odd, cholesterol-conscious meal: a grilled chicken sandwich from McDonald's (hold the special sauce); ten Pringles potato chips (baked, not fried); a banana; a serving of fruit compote that she had cooked, usually strawberries; and two cookies. Served in that order. Henry looked forward to our visits because he loves to eat. He's not much of a talker and would send us on our way when he was done.

But I was no less the beneficiary of these outings. Most of the time when I picked my mother up at the Metro station, she would be schlepping one or two heavy shopping bags filled with containers of food she'd cooked and frozen for me. My freezer was always stocked with her chicken *matzo*-ball soup, chopped liver, stuffed cabbage, beef stew, *mandelbrot*, and apple pie. She made her piecrust on a wooden board the old-fashioned way—a big pile of flour with a well in the center into which she worked the eggs, sugar, and butter to make her dough. She was a great cook, having learned a lot working with Sabina in the kitchen in Ulm and developing a natural facility for it over the years. She refused to believe it, though. She still defined herself by her reputation as a terrible cook from when she burned the coffee at Zionist youth camp. But good cook or bad, feeding her children was one of her highest priorities.

One Sunday after we had visited my brother, she and I took ourselves out to lunch. The restaurant was crowded and we faced a half-hour wait. However, there was room at the bar. My mother, who was never more than five foot two to begin with, was by then quite tiny and couldn't get onto the bar stool from a standing position. She tried to hoist herself up by putting one foot onto the rung of the chair but lacked the strength to follow through. So I got behind her and, with one arm under each of her armpits, I lifted her onto the stool. Then I pushed the chair close in to the bar. It was like putting a baby in a high chair.

Boy, did we laugh.

2007: Final Days

My mother's greatest gift to me was that she didn't merely survive but truly lived, in keeping with her highest ideals and values. Her life was precious to her and she fought for it—but only on her terms. Some years earlier a sniper was terrorizing Washington at Metro stations. She preferred riding the Metro to driving when she could, but under the circumstances, I suggested maybe she should avoid the Metro for the time being. She said, "I don't want to live that way." I didn't say another word.

My mother retained an outer beauty reflecting a natural inner grace. She was blessed with excellent health and an uncommonly youthful appearance, sharp intellect, and physical vitality. And a gentle, sensitive nature of such sweetness that endured despite the extraordinary hardships she'd suffered.

Over time, my mother lost most of those close to her but remained healthy, fit, and self-sufficient. She always said that she was in no rush for whatever lay ahead, but neither would she wish to return to some younger age. Even at ninety she still lived alone in her own home, did most of her housework, and drove her car. Notwithstanding her disclaimers about lack of skill in the kitchen, she was a wonderful cook and never lost the instinct to feed her children. Where as a child I had resisted her efforts to make me eat, as an adult I felt blessed that she still stocked my freezer with all the Old World comfort foods of my childhood.

Around this time, the same kind of serendipity and uncanny coincidence that so often punctuated my mother's life played out in my random meeting with Planaria Price, the writer of this book. I was vacationing with a friend in Big Sur, California, and we went out for dinner. Because of a fierce storm few people had ventured out and the restaurant was almost empty. Marcia and I sat at the bar and started chatting with the only other people there, Planaria Price and her husband, Murray Burns.

It was the kind of evening when the chef was sending out free food and conversation flowed. We learned that Planaria was a teacher of English as a Second Language from Los Angeles. She wasn't acquainted with my childhood friend Rena Horowitz, who also teaches English as a Second Language in Los Angeles, but Rena, whom I called later that evening, was quite familiar with her. "You met Planaria Price? She's phenomenal! I attend her workshops whenever I can and have all of her books. I'm so impressed you met her."

By then the four of us had already become fast friends. As we got to know one another Planaria became intrigued with my mother's story. "This should be a book," she said, to which I replied, "I think so, too, but it's more than I'm about to take on." "I'll write it!" she exclaimed. A few weeks later, back home in DC, I followed up by sending Planaria a DVD shot ten years earlier of my mother telling her story. We both wanted to be sure it hadn't just been the wine talking.

I presented my mother with what I thought was a gift: that someone wanted to write a book about her life. She saw nothing in herself or her story special enough to merit a book. While she'd always taken herself seriously, she lacked any sense of self-importance. But she agreed to the project as a gift to me.

A few months into this process, Planaria twice coming to Washington, DC, to interview my mother and sending me questions to explore with her, my mother was diagnosed with non-Hodgkins lymphoma. For the better part of one year, as she underwent fairly mild chemotherapy treatments, she and I spent precious hours together gathering the information and memories that have become this book. Her remarkable memory for descriptive and narrative detail and self-awareness of her inner life fueled Planaria's intuitive vision in a way that seemed almost channeled.

One example: Planaria wanted to know if my mother could describe her first-grade teacher, even what she wore on the first day of school, if she could remember. That my mother did remember was amazing enough. But when I started to pass her answer on, Planaria stopped me short and said, "Wait. Here's what I see. She's tall and thin, has light brown hair that she wears in a bun and light eyes. She's wearing a gray dress with brown dots and a gold crucifix on a chain around her neck." The only part that deviated from my mother's description was the color of the dots. They were black.

For all her happy memories of growing up in Piotrków, or probably because of them, my mother never wanted to go back there. But I did. And several months into our conversations for this book, I had the chance.

In August 2007, my cousin Irving Gomolin (Idek's son), his daughter Molly, and I attended a reunion in Piotrków for the families of Jewish survivors from the town. The occasion was a ceremony at the Jewish cemetery to dedicate a crypt containing the sacred writings that Naphtali Lau had risked his life at the start of the war to rescue from the Great Synagogue and bury before they could be destroyed. Naphtali and his youngest brother, Yisrael, were the only members of Rebbitzin Lau's family to survive, and I was honored to meet them in Piotrków.

Naphtali saved his and his young brother's lives while they were in Buchenwald. They made *aliyah* (immigration) to Israel after the war. Naphtali was eighteen and grew up to become top aide to Moshe Dayan and participated in the Camp David peace talks, when Anwar Sadat and Menachem Begin made history by ending the state of war between Egypt and Israel. He ended his career as Ambassador Lau-Lavie, Israeli Consul to New York. Yisrael, eight when he was liberated, grew up to become the chief Ashkenazi rabbi of Israel and head of Yad Vashem, the World Holocaust Remembrance Center in Jerusalem. Both men came to know many of the world's top leaders, movie stars, and even the Pope.

I knew of Naphtali because as chairman of the Claims Committee, working for restitution to Holocaust survivors of private property seized by the Nazis, he and my mother had corresponded over the years. She had documentation of her family's ownership of the building at 21 Piłsudskiego Street, where they had both grown up. Naphtali told me that my mother was his most significant connection to that part of his life. He had been close friends with her younger sister, Regina, and told me that he had loved her. And he shared a few memories of my mother and her friendship with the rebbitzin. It wasn't until a few years later that I learned of my father's role in helping him survive in the labor camp, when I read about it in Naphtali's autobiography, *Balaam's Prophecy*. This connection from the past and a natural affinity forged an ongoing connection with him and his wife, Joan. Naphtali died in 2014.

During this powerfully affecting trip to Piotrków, my cousins and I, though we knew our family home had been torn down, went to see the empty lot at 21 Piłsudskiego. The city of Piotrków is now designated on the deed as owner of the property. Poland has the worst record in all of Europe for restoring what had been stolen from their Jewish citizens. The argument is that the Germans, not the Poles, committed the war crimes of confiscating the property, so Poland is not responsible for compensating the rightful Jewish owners. There has been restitution in recent years for Jewish community property, the orphanage, the community center, etc., but not for private homes. Though it is possible, in theory, for Jews to reclaim their homes. All they need to do is return to live in them or pay all back taxes since the war. In other words, not. The Great Synagogue in Piotrków, bullet holes still visible in the walls, is now the public library. With no Jews left in the town to worship there, it's probably just as well. At least it hasn't been left to fall into ruin or be demolished.

Yet it's also true that the mayor and city government couldn't be more encouraging and supportive of our Jewish reunions there every few years. They help organize our visits, and during the day or two before our arrival they conduct programs to teach the schoolchildren about what happened and why we're there. These interesting, complicated, seemingly contradictory impulses play out all over Europe, where anti-Semitism is on the rise (yet again) and at the same time where many people are trying to understand and commemorate their own loss of the Jewish communities that had been such a rich, distinctive, and colorful part of their national histories. But there are no Jews left to inform their mythologies, that's the whole point. And so many of the most sincere efforts at honoring this extinct world, like the lively, hip, restored, old Jewish section of Kazimierz in Kraków, come across like Disneyland.

The key event at our reunion was the ceremony at the memorial in the Rakow Forest, where during the liquidation the Germans shot hundreds of the Jews they had rounded up, fifty at a time. Standing alone at the edge of our gathering was a tiny, birdlike man who had bicycled over, wearing a suit too large for him. Clearly he had dressed up out of respect for the occasion. I learned this was a local Pole who as a fifteen-year-old peasant had witnessed the executions and now, sixty-five years later, this unassuming, uneducated old man had the heart to join us. I cannot recall this image without choking up.

My final moment in Piotrków: everyone was on the bus but I had to run back to where we had lunched to retrieve some papers I'd left there. We had taken over and brought in kosher food to the restaurant on Rynek Trybunalski, the main square where my father's family had their business, where my mother and Heniek and all the townsfolk took their evening *shpetzias*. The place was empty, except for the chief rabbi of Poland (an American), who'd been part of our event, and the two Polish barmaids, their glasses of schnapps raised in a toast.

Shortly after I returned from that trip we learned that my mother's treatments hadn't worked. Over the next two months her medical condition worsened, and after three weeks in the hospital it was clear that she wasn't going to get better. As her pain increased I had to coach her on how to act when she was ready to ask for something stronger than Tylenol, so unnatural was it for her to say "I need something." Up until then her only replies to "How are you feeling?" were "Fine" or "Much better." ("Much better than what? You were fine!")

We talked openly and sometimes even joked about everything that was happening. One afternoon in the hospital, out of the blue she said to me, "Don't put my age in the obituary." She was ninety-one.

I said, "But if someone asks me afterward how old you were, what am I supposed to say? 'I don't know'?"

She thought for a moment, then replied, "Say eighty-nine."

I frankly don't know whether this was motivated by a quirky kind of vanity or an irrational fear that I could get in trouble for some ancient monkey business with her birthdate on her legal documentation for entering the United States. But it cracked me up.

Until her last moments my mother remained true to herself and never lowered her standards. Her doctor remarked that it was almost unique in his experience for someone facing their own mortality to seem more concerned with the needs and feelings of others. The day before she died, she was groaning in pain. While I was on the phone trying urgently to reach her doctor, she was pressing me to charge her cell phone battery so that I'd have a backup, wanting to spare me my frustration when I'd let mine run down.

But when she understood that living an independent existence would no longer be possible, she was ready to let go. She lived a long life, self-determined to the end, and triumphed by dying according to the laws of nature, not of Hitler. My mother held on until just after midnight on the 13th, as she'd done when delivering me, and at 12:30 a.m. on October 14, 2007, my mother met her end, unafraid.

WHAT HAPPENED TO THE OTHERS

THE GOMOLINSKI FAMILY

Itzak Hirsch Gomolinski: Died in Treblinka Concentration Camp.

Hendla Libeskind Gomolinska: Died of typhus in the Piotrków ghetto, July 1941.

Hela: Survived Bugaj Labor Camp and Ravensbrück and Bergen-Belsen concentration camps with her eight-year-old son, **Marek**. In 1947 she and Marek immigrated to Haifa (then Palestine) to reunite with her husband, **Jacob Brem**, who had survived the war serving as a conscript in the Soviet army. He died in 1967. Hela died in 2007. **Marek** (now **Moshe**) is now living in Haifa. In 1943, Hela's brother-in-law, **Abek Brem**, who was instrumental in Basia's first escape attempt, was taken by the Nazis to Rakow Forest outside of Piotrków with others and shot.

Chanusck: Died in infancy.

Idek: Survived imprisonment in Bugaj Labor Camp and Buchenwald Concentration Camp. Immigrated to Montreal, Canada, after the war. He died in 1996.

Josek: Survived Bugaj Labor Camp, then escaped into the forest in transit to Buchenwald. After the Liberation, he was severely injured in a car accident. When he recovered, he immigrated to Montreal, Canada. He died in 1998.

Beniek: Died in Treblinka Concentration Camp.

Rifka: Died in infancy.

Regina: Died in Treblinka Concentration Camp.

OTHER FAMILIES FEATURED IN THE STORY

Uncle Josef Libeskind (Hendla's brother, Basia's uncle): Survived the war hidden by a gentile family in Warsaw. Immigrated to Israel afterward.

Aunt Sura Libeskind: Hidden for a time with a gentile family in Warsaw, who were then denounced by a neighbor. She and they all died in Auschwitz.

Janek: Survived the war by passing as a Pole and living with a gentile family in Warsaw. After Liberation he immigrated to Paris. Janek is responsible for saving the lives of his family members who did survive.

Mala: With forged papers, passed as a gentile in Germany, escaped to Switzerland, then immigrated to Israel after the war.

Mania: Passed as a gentile in Warsaw, immigrated to Israel after the war.

Mendel: Survived the war with his wife, **Genia,** and their son, **Shlomo,** passing as gentiles in Warsaw. Settled in Israel after the war and died of leukemia soon after. When a teenager, Shlomo immigrated to the United States and is currently a professor of mathematics in Oregon.

Moshe: Survived Bergen-Belsen Concentration Camp, then immigrated to Ramat Gan, Israel.

Rozia: Died in a concentration camp.

Uncle Mendel (Hendla's brother, Basia's uncle) and **Aunt Sprintza Libeskind:** Died with four of their five children, including **Hinda,** in a concentration camp.

Elkanah: The only member of the family to survive, after imprisonment in Hortensja Labor Camp and Buchenwald Concentration Camp. He moved to Philadelphia, where he died shortly thereafter.

Rabbi Moshe Chaim Lau: Died in Treblinka Concentration Camp.

Rebbitzin Chaya Lau: Died in Ravensbrück Concentration Camp.

Naphtali (Tulek): Survived, while protecting his young brother, Yisrael, in Hortensja Labor Camp and Buchenwald Concentration Camp. Immigrated to Israel, where he became a journalist, and later a diplomat serving as Moshe Dayan's top aide and as a participant in the Camp David peace talks with Anwar Sadat. He ended his career as the Israeli consul general in New York. He died in 2014.

Shmuel Yitzhak (Milek): Worked in the Hortensja Labor Camp, but unfortunately stayed home with his parents on the day of the ghetto deportations and was sent with his father to Treblinka, where he was killed.

Yisrael (Lulek): Protected by his brother Naphtali, survived Hortensja Labor Camp and Buchenwald Concentration Camp. Immigrated to Israel, where he grew up to become the chief Ashkenazi rabbi from 1993 to 2003. He is now the chief rabbi of Tel Aviv and the chairman of Yad Vashem.

Baila Reichmann (Leon Reichmann's mother): She and five of her six children died in Buchenwald. Only her son **Leon** (Basia's husband) survived the war.

Abraham Reichmann (Leon Reichmann's brother): The first Jew to be killed in Piotrków for not obeying curfew.

Henry Marton (Leon Reichmann's cousin): Survived Hortensja Labor Camp and settled after the war in Asbury Park, New Jersey.

Heniek Wajshof (Basia's high school boyfriend): Died in Treblinka Concentration Camp together with his parents, his sister **Dora**, and his new wife, **Maryla**.

Mania Wajshof (Heniek Wajshof's sister): Survived the war.

Srulek Wajshof (Heniek Wajshof's cousin): Escaped to Russia and survived. After the war he settled in Netanya, Israel.

OTHER MAIN CHARACTERS

Itka Ber (Basia's childhood friend): Died in a concentration camp.

Itka Moskowitz (Basia's college roomate): Died in a concentration camp.

Rozia Nissenson (Basia's school friend): Survived a concentration camp, settled in Haifa, Israel.

Sabina Sheratska, née **Markowitz** (Barbara's wartime companion): Died in Munich, Germany, two years after the war from an infection four days after giving birth. Her husband, **Abram Altus**, and one-year-old son, **Joel**, immigrated to Detroit, Michigan. Joel now lives in Seattle, Washington. One of his children is a daughter named **Sabina**.

Sala Grinzspan (Basia's school friend): Left Poland before the war to study at the Technion University in Haifa, Israel, where she made her home after the war.

Sala Jacobowitz Reichmann (Leon Reichmann's first wife): Killed with her newborn daughter after leaving the Piotrków ghetto to give birth in the Catholic hospital, where she was denounced as a Jew.

GLOSSARY

Ach, wunderbar (German): Oh, wonderful

Aktion (German): Non-military action to further Nazi ideals of race; generally refers to the assembly and deportation of Jews to concentration or death camps

Arbeitsampt (German): Employment agency set up by the Germans in Poland for Poles to find work in Germany

babushka (Russian): Grandmother

borscht (Russian/Yiddish): Soup made from beets

challah (Hebrew/Yiddish): Jewish braided egg bread served on Sabbath and holidays

charoset (Hebrew): One of the symbolic Passover Seder foods; made of chopped apples, almonds, raisins, cinnamon, and wine; symbolizes the mortar the Jews had to make when they were slaves of Pharaoh

cholent (Yiddish): A casserole, generally made of meat and beans or potatoes; cooked overnight and usually eaten on the Sabbath

chuppa (Hebrew): Ritual marriage canopy held over the bride and groom

davening (Yiddish): Praying, facing in the direction of Jerusalem; done three times a day

Diaspora (Greek): Historical mass involuntary dispersion, such as the expulsion of the Jews from Judea

dobra (Polish): Good

DP camp: Refugee camp for displaced persons

Eretz Yisrael (Hebrew): The land of Israel, the Jewish Holy Land

gefilte fish (Yiddish): Ground carp made into balls or small cakes

gentile (English): Non-Jew

Haggadah (Hebrew): The book read at the Passover Seder that tells the story of the Exodus of the Jews from Egypt, and also contains instructions for conducting the Seder service

Hasid (Hebrew): Member of a branch of Orthodox Judaism that promotes spirituality through a popularization of Jewish teachings, especially mysticism; founded in Eastern Europe in the eighteenth century

HIAS (English): Hebrew Immigrant Aid Society

Judenrat (German): Council of Jews in the ghetto

Judenrein (German): Free of Jews

Kaddish (Hebrew): Mourners' prayer

Kennkarte (German): Official identification card

kibbutz (Hebrew): Agricultural commune in Israel

kosher (Hebrew): Satisfying the guidelines of Jewish law

kugel (Yiddish): Baked noodle dish

kvuca (Hebrew): Term for the small groups into which members of Zionist groups were divided

landsman (Yiddish): Fellow Jew

Lebensraum (German): Living space

machzor (Hebrew): Prayer book used by Jews on the High Holidays of Rosh Hashanah and Yom Kippur

Mamashi (Yiddish): "My mama"

mandelbrot (Yiddish): Almond cookies popular among Eastern European Jews

maror (Hebrew): Bitter herbs, e.g., horseradish, eaten during the Seder, alludes to the bitterness of the lives of the Jews as slaves of Pharaoh in Egypt

matzo (Hebrew): Unleavened bread eaten during Passover; *matzot* plural

matzo balls: Dumplings made from matzo meal and served in chicken soup

Mein Kampf (German): *My Struggle*, manifesto published by Adolf Hitler in 1925

mezuzah (Hebrew): Small decorative scroll containing Torah excerpts placed on the door frame of a home; *mezuzot* plural

minyan (Hebrew): Group of at least ten Jewish men; the smallest number who may say certain communal prayers

Mensch (German/Yiddish): Upright, honest, decent person

mitzvah (Hebrew): Torah commandment; also used to mean a good deed; *mitzvot* plural

ouroboros (Greek): Ancient circular symbol of a serpent swallowing its tail, representing the message of renewal, infinity, and wholeness in the cyclic nature of the universe

Paschal Lamb: The Passover Lamb, eaten on the first night of the holiday with bitter herbs and *matzo*

Pesach (Hebrew/Yiddish): The eight-day spring holiday of Passover

Rosh Hashanah (Hebrew): Jewish New Year

Schnell! (German): Hurry up!

Seder (Hebrew): The ritual meal that begins the eight-day celebration of Passover

Shabbos (Yiddish): The Sabbath, a day of religious observance from sundown on Friday night to shortly after sundown on Saturday night

shiva (Hebrew): Traditional seven days of mourning

shochet (Yiddish): The ritual slaughterer, who kills animals for butchers according to Jewish law

shpetzia (Yiddish): Walking outside with friends

siddur (Hebrew): Jewish prayer book

SS (German): *Schutzstaffel* ("Protective Squadron")—part of the Nazi army, particularly involved in carrying out the Holocaust

tatte (Yiddish): Papa, an endearment

tikkun olam (Hebrew): Healing the world

Torah (Hebrew): The Hebrew Bible

Volksdeutsche (German): Ethnic German living in another country, e.g., Poland

Wehrmacht (German): The unified armed forces of Germany from 1935 to 1945

wojna (Polish): War

yarmulke (Yiddish): Skullcap worn especially during prayer or religious study by Jewish males

Yom Kippur (Hebrew): The Day of Atonement; ten days after Rosh Hashanah

zayde (Yiddish): Grandfather

Zhid (Polish): Jew

zloty (Polish): The basic currency unit of Poland

ACKNOWLEDGMENTS

PLANARIA PRICE

This book owes its inception and completion to Helen West, who shared her mother's story with me, and who invited me to meet and interview her ninety-year-old mother, Barbara, in Washington, DC. Through this twelve-year project, Helen has been my partner in every aspect of creating and developing this book. In particular she has been invaluable in assuring the accuracy of this biography, introducing me to family members, and helping to tweak my sentences and choice of words to echo Barbara's voice.

My deepest gratitude to Barbara (Basia) Reichmann, who lovingly let me into her life and shared her most intimate memories with me, both the joy and the pain.

The warmest of thank-yous to Ronna Magy, who patiently listened to my whining, year in, year out, about not being able to find an agent, and for her suggestion that I contact Erica Silverman who, not even knowing me, spent copious amounts of time to counsel, advise, and encourage me and who suggested I contact the Deborah Harris Agency. Thank you to George Eltman of that agency, who so carefully polished the manuscript, and to our wonderful agent, Rena Rossner, who introduced this book to Farrar Straus Giroux. Rena has always been there to advise and support.

A most deep, heartfelt thank-you to our brilliant, understanding, and patient editors at FSG, first Susan Dobinick, and then Wesley Adams and his assistant, Megan Abbate, for eagle-eyed editing, marvelous advice, warm support, and for believing in this project.

Gratitude to Dr. David H. Lindquist, co-director of the Indiana

University, Purdue, Institute for Holocaust and Genocide Studies, for his extremely reinforcing review of the first draft. His very positive feedback gave me the strength to go forward.

Kudos to my earliest readers for their warm encouragement and wonderful editing suggestions: Bradford Richardson (the very first to read), Judith Simon Prager, Diane Pershing, Euphronia Awakuni, and Mark Thaler.

It is with sadness that, with the passing of Ben Giladi, I cannot personally thank him for his help and the richness of the information in *The Voice of Piotrków Survivors*. I wish I could tell him how much his intensive research helped me to keep the memories alive.

The deepest of thank-yous to Moshe (Marek) Brem for sharing his moving story with me and to his wife, Aliza, for her lovely translation of Marek's words.

Thanks to Michael Schwarber, my computer guru, for saving my sanity and the manuscript.

It is my fervent hope that after reading the story of Basia and Sabina, young adults of today will work for *tikkun olam*, trying to repair the world, and fighting against all genocides and horrors in our future.

HELEN REICHMANN WEST

Planaria Price—alchemist, artist, magician, storyteller—you have my boundless gratitude. Through your uncanny vision and freewheeling imagination, you transformed the raw ingredients of my mother's memories into a living presence and brought a vibrant world back to life. Following your lead as we've worked together over these twelve years, I've been in awe of your unflagging energy for fine-tuning, polishing, and refining this book. Your dogged determination and unquestioning faith that this book would find a home have been inspirational.

On her ninetieth birthday, just a few weeks after my mother agreed to proceed with this book, she commented on my friendships, observing, "You're all so lucky. You're like family but you like each other!" I am deeply touched by the gift of true friendship from my family of choice, and give particular thanks to Marcia Litman Greene, Molly Pauker, Steve Shere, and David Waldman for your enthusiastic engagement in this project and your honest, insightful, and invaluable critiques every step of the way. What good luck that my dearest friends happen also to be such thoughtful, sophisticated, and sensitive readers.

Of the remaining family I am lucky to have been born into, thanks to my cousins Irving Gomolin, Moshe (Marek) Brem, Shlomo Libeskind, and Sarah (Mrs. Henry) Marton. You are part of this story. You knew and loved my mother and helped keep this rendering real. To my friends and gifted writers Bettie Banks and Del McNeely, you didn't know my mother and helped keep this story true.

I wish Naphtali Lau-Lavie and Ben Giladi, friends and admirers of my mother when they were young people in Piotrków, were still with us. I would thank them for extending their friendship to me and for their contributions to our re-creation here of the rich world they all once shared. Thanks, too, to Jacek Bednajac of Piotrków, Poland, for your research into the archives and your devotion to honoring the former Jewish community there. Ann Elkington, your feeling for my mother and her story found artful expression in the maps you created for inclusion in this book.

Thanks to our agents at the Deborah Harris Agency, George Eltman and Rena Rossner, who believed in this book, knew where it belonged, and knew how to get it there; to Susan Dobinick, who started us on our way by acquiring this book for Farrar Straus Giroux; and to Wesley Adams and Megan Abbate, our editors at FSG, who got the value, the point, and the voice and who seamlessly brought this book to full maturity, ready to launch.

And finally, thanks to Carl Frank, brilliant writer and talented literary critic. Your lovingly ruthless standards for excellence give extra weight to your belief and delight in this book. But most of all, thank you for giving my mother peace at the end, knowing I have you. Her most deeply held value, instilled in me through lesson and by example, was to care for good character above all else, in myself and in the people I choose for companions. I remember as a young child wondering how I would find my mate when I grew up and imagining that my mother would guide me. She chose you.

PHOTO CREDITS

Unless otherwise indicated, images are from the collection of Barbara Reichmann, courtesy of Helen Reichmann West. Grateful acknowledgment is extended to Helen and to the following: Frontispiece, page ii: University of Kraków. Photo insert, page 1: (top) Museum of the History of Polish Jews, Warsaw, (bottom) Yad Vashem; page 2: (top) Piotrków Trybunalski government archives; page 3: (top) The New York Public Library, Yiddish Book Center Yizkor Book Collection, (bottom) Piotrków Trybunalski government archives; page 4: (top row) Shai Lau-Lavie, (middle row and bottom) Piotrków Trybunalski government archives; page 5: (top) Photo12/UIG via Getty Images, (bottom) Chris Webb; page 6: (top and bottom) holocaustresearchproject.org; page 7: (top) wikipedia.org, (bottom right) Moshe and Aliza Brem; page 8: (top) United States Holocaust Memorial Museum, courtesy of Ben Jachimowicz James; page 10: (bottom) © The Israel Museum, Jerusalem, photograph by Tim (Nahum) Gidal (1909–96); page 15: (bottom) Shai Lau-Lavie.